Law, Enlightenment, and Other States of Mind

Kevin Rhodes

ISBN: 0989097005
ISBN 13: 9780989097000

eBooks by Kevin Rhodes:

Life Beyond Reason: A Memoir of Mania
Not This Day! Special Features
(with co-author Gillian Rhodes)
Law, Enlightenment, and Other States of Mind

FROM THE EDITOR

Every Thursday, the Colorado Bar Association CLE Legal Connection blog features one of Kevin Rhodes' inspirational posts. And every Wednesday, I get a little jump of excitement when Kevin emails his post to me for the next day – I get a sneak peek.

I look forward to reading Kevin's posts. They are a welcome reprieve from the usual case law or rule change articles. I feel connected to Kevin because of these little glimpses into his personality – the warm, accepting, mentally healthy individual that comes through in his articles.

Besides being fun to read, Kevin's posts serve an important role in this era where lawyer depression has reached nearly epidemic proportions. Kevin imparts a bit of humanity – a bit of total wellbeing – into his writing, and I can only hope that lawyers struggling with depression and dark thoughts are able to find a little light in his writing. I know I do.

Susan Hoyt
Legal Editor/Social Media
Colorado Bar Association CLE

CONTENTS

FOREWORD

by Ronald M. Sandgrund, Esq.
After thirty-plus years as a trial lawyer and managing partner of a boutique Denver law firm, while also moonlighting as an author of articles for new and experienced attorneys regarding the ups and downs and ins and outs of practicing law, I very much looked forward to reading Kevin Rhodes' regular Colorado Bar Association essays. When I began researching potential persons to interview for *Is There a Better Exit Strategy Than Death?*, an article I assembled for the August 2014 issue of *The Colorado Lawyer,* Kevin was at the top of my list. He graciously agreed to meet me downtown for coffee and, before I knew what hit me, I was pulled into the vortex of laughter and smarts that is Hurricane Kevin. How terrific to find all of Kevin's blog posts assembled in one place -- contemplative chicken soup for the soul!

Drawing on his professional and personal sojourn through that minefield called life, and with inestimable wit and wisdom, Kevin offers advice, humor and insight to Colorado lawyers and anyone else who is willing to take just a few *moments* out of their day to stop and *listen* and *think.* To folks cobbled by the seemingly endless demands of work, Kevin's decision to leave his law practice and develop a Broadway musical may seem puzzling, if not downright crazy. But, for anyone who has pursued a dream, taken a chance, engaged in a leap of faith, or thrown the dice, Kevin was doing no more than living life fully.

This book amuses, amazes and edifies just as the original blog posts did when I read them in real time over the past few years. I knew then I was hearing a fun and lively voice calling into the dark wilderness that can too often surround and suffocate otherwise creative spirits.

Kevin's book journeys us through Inspiration, Change, Accountability and Personal Apocalypses but, ultimately leads us to Transformation. He speaks with a big heart and from a great breadth of experience. Every lawyer – every one of us – can learn from Kevin's acute observations about the need to be "entrepreneurial," not just in our business affairs and professional pursuits, but with our families and our own wellness. My favorite piece concerned "change without judgment," and not being afraid to "want what you want." This essay really resonated: too many good and talented people I have known were afraid to want what they wanted, and were afraid of change for fear they would be judged. To them I say, "Let Kevin show you the way."

Ronald M. Sandgrund

FOREWORD

by Debra S. Austin, J.D., Ph. D.

Kevin Rhodes is an audacious man. In this book, he dares us to be audacious right along with him.

Kevin asks us to become self-reflective. He challenges us to question the status quo and he urges us to reinvent ourselves. He explains how we can get stuck and he offers a path forward. In short, Kevin empowers growth.

An idea that connects Kevin's work with my work is a fervent belief that we can do better. We can live better lives and we can create better cultures. In a society that has been constructed around the black and white principles of success and failure, Kevin redirects us to consider how we can grow and change.

I have been thinking about growth and change, in terms of improving learning and teaching, for my entire career: first as a middle school teacher; then as a law student; a corporate trainer; an education doctoral student; and law professor. Kevin and I are both synthesizers of research and of ideas. We bring important information to busy people. I am honored that Kevin chose to think about, highlight, and bring his impassioned insight to my law journal article *Killing Them Softly*, in which I wrote about the neuroscience of learning and the impact of stress on cognition, and offered recommendations for improving brain health.

Kevin reminds us that the pursuit of growth and change is an imprecise, and often scary endeavor. But each of his short essays prods and coaches on the benefits of taking brave steps to effect growth and change. We can design better cultures and curate better lives. This can become our new normal. Kevin advises it takes perseverance, courage, and intensity to improve humanity. And science, too.

In one of his *Running Past Our Limits* posts, Kevin invites us to acknowledge the "kid's soul living in an adult's body" that each of us has within ourselves, which may be his best tip for empowering growth and change in his readers. Let Kevin awaken your "kid's soul!"

Debra S. Austin
Lawyering Process Professor,
University of Denver Law School

LAWYERS ARE PEOPLE, TOO

I don't know who reads my blog. The Colorado Bar Association doesn't know either. Or maybe they choose not to know. The legal profession is good at confidentiality.

I know that my readers almost never post comments, which for awhile made me think I didn't have any, until my editor kindly assured me otherwise. Every once in a blue moon somebody emails me about a post. I'll take that. Someone out there read it. I'm happy.

It's because of those emails that I know not all my readers are lawyers. They are brave people, those non-lawyer readers: they have to cross a minefield of professional incomprehensibility to get what they're looking for.

But lawyers are people, too, just like those non-lawyers. Ultimately that's who I write for, and who reads my blog: people. Some are lawyers, some are not, but all of them are people, lawyer jokes aside.

True, the blog serves up topics in packages of particular interest to lawyers -- it's sponsored by the Colorado Bar Association, after all. But once the package is opened, the posts go looking for people, lawyer or not, who want to create or at least embrace change in their workplaces and personal lives. And not just change, but transformation -- the biggest, boldest kind of change.

The shared human experiences of noticing, wanting, aspiring, committing, suffering, accomplishing (or not), celebrating (or not)... those are the experiences I'm after. I'm also after experiences that are none of those things, when disasters crash into our lives and we have no choice but to deal. I want to know how we grow and change and transform our way through all those kinds of experiences. And I want to know how getting through them affects our professional and personal lives every day.

The CBA lets me write about these things, and for that, I'm constantly amazed and grateful.

Kevin Rhodes

A BLOG GROWS UP

P utting this collection together, it's been interesting to see how the posts have changed in both content and form in the past three years.

For one thing, they've gotten leggier. I started with a self-imposed word target of 375 that jumped to 500; several of the posts in the final series in this collection are pushing 600+. The series got longer, too: they started at two or three posts, settled in at six, flirted with seven, and the last one weighs in at eight. (It has a lot to say, that final *Killing Them Softly* series. More on that in a moment.)

In the beginning, the posts mostly recycled material from what would become my book *Life Beyond Reason: A Memoir of Mania*, which is sort of the unabridged version of *The Colorado Lawyer* interview Ron Sandgrund told you about in his Foreword. *Life Beyond Reason* is about how I left a successful law career to produce a stage show, got way more than I bargained for, and ended up a changed man. The book is my personal operating system, and I still quote it now and then.

Eventually, the posts began to reach beyond my own reflections. They weren't just test driving my ideas anymore, they were reaching out to a world full of fascinating people doing fascinating things, people engaged in significant research and hands-on experiments with the goal of making our work and personal lives friendlier to the human soul. I'd found the mother lode, and started digging, dazzled by all the gems.

Fired with that energy, the posts hit a new stride right about the *Are Lawyers Unhappy?* series. Susan Hoyt, my editor now and at that time, told me that, during that series, there were days when a quarter of the hits to the *Legal Connection* site went straight to the blog. Obviously we'd struck a nerve. (Susan also wondered what I was smoking when I followed up with the *Morphic Fields* series, which generated some of the more entertaining reader emails I've gotten.)

Then along came a gift: the *2013 Colorado Lawyer Salary and Satisfaction Survey.* Suddenly I had real live research in my own backyard, plus real live people I could talk to about it. My world (not to mention my LinkedIn connections) expanded, and so did the column's content. My personal interests in psychology. neuroscience, creativity, innovation, and entrepreneurship got a boost as I was inspired to deepen my research, and find new ways to connect it to the blog.

About then, two additional developments further ramped up the blog's energy: (1) we shifted to weekly instead of twice a month, and (2) I discovered the joy of hyperlinks. Thanks to the latter, I had a non-stuffy way to cite all those new sources I was discovering, and could also invite readers to go further exploring on their own. I have no idea how much those links get used, but it makes me happy just to know they're there. They make the blog more of an audience participation event, and I like that. (Of course all the hyperlinks are deleted in this print edition. If you want to know where to find a story or article I cite, or a specific term, you can email me, and I'll send you a link if there was one in the original post.)

The finale to this collection, *Killing Them Softly*, is maybe the best example of how the blog has changed since it started. Prof. Austin's comprehensive work on the neuroscience of lawyer cognition gathered much of what I'd written about, supersized it, packaged it in a giant box, and stamped it with a string of big exclamation points. Writing that series was like working on a college senior comps project: going back to find threads of learning, tracing them through the years, weaving them together into a new level of comprehension, and realizing that there's a whole lot more out there left to be discovered.

How appropriate, then, that the last post in that series, and in this collection, is the 98th I've written. According to numerologists, 99 is a number of perfect completion. If so, then this collection is one post shy of a complete blog. I'm okay with that. Hitting the magic number 99 would have been nice, but ending at completion wouldn't have suited where the blog has been or how it prefers to travel. It seems to like its own raggedness, and I like that about it.

Once the blog finally does hit that magic 99th post, it will be both an arrival and a departure, a wrap up of what's gone before and an invitation to what's next. Nice. I didn't plan it that way, but nice. Completion and arriving are satisfying -- they burn like a friendly fireplace -- but anticipation of what might be coming next is the red sky at morn' that wakes you up to new, glorious, and scary possibilities just made for exploring. Both coming home and leaving have their places, but I confess there's something inside of me that thinks setting out on a new adventure is about as good as it gets.

In fact, that's been the most remarkable and consistent aspect of writing these posts: it's always an adventure, always unpredictable, always dangerous. Just when I think I've got nothing new to write about, the posts themselves shed the next light I need to keep going. They lure me onward, awaken me to new discoveries, invite me on new adventures.

Writing them enhances not just my understanding, but my experience of life.

I hope reading them has the same effect on you.

WANT CHANGE?
BE UNREASONABLE

(Part 1 of 3)

I f we want to create something new in our lives – a new career, a new relationship, a new firm, whatever – then we can't be reasonable about it. That's a tough idea to swallow for people who make their living being eminently reasonable.

We can agree that George Bernard Shaw was a reasonable man, right? But listen to what he said about this:

> The reasonable man adapts himself to the world; the unreasonable one persists in trying to adapt the world to himself. Therefore, all progress depends on the unreasonable man.
>
> *From* Maxims for Revolutionaries

"All progress depends on the unreasonable man." Why? Because reason can only look backward. It makes sense of what is and what has been. The trouble is, *new*, by definition, is what hasn't yet been. Therefore reason doesn't know about it, doesn't understand it, can't trust it.

Reason is all about precedent. It can only project and extrapolate. It looks at where we are now and how we got here, then projects its conclusions into the future, reverse engineering what happened in the past so we can do more of it in the future.

We call people who think like that realists – reasonable people – and credit them with being more in touch with reality than daydreamers and visionaries. We trust them not to lead us astray.

But what if we want to be and do something we haven't yet been and done? What if we're inspired to do something new?

Inspiration isn't at all reasonable. It wants idealists, not realists. It wants people who are consumed with an idea about what could be, not what is. People like that don't give a rip about reverse engineering. Instead, they buy what Einstein said about imagination being more powerful than knowledge. They're willing to push boundaries, believe what's considered irrational, illogical, impossible, even irreverent and heretical.

Inspiration wants response, not reason. It hooks our hearts, then reels us in. Want change? First get hooked by an inspired idea. Then get unreasonable.

WANT CHANGE?
FIRST, CHANGE EVERYTHING

(Part 2 of 3)

Inspiration is strong energy. It comes asking the impossible – impossible not just because of the task to be done, but also because of who's asked to do it. *Especially* who's asked to do it.

Inspiration speaks with such conviction that we rarely doubt its ideas and visions. If we're going to doubt anything, we're going to doubt ourselves. But, despite what we think, we are *always* the most qualified candidate for our dreams. Big Ideas come to claim their own. If it's my idea, dream, vision, then only one person gets to be its champion: me.

Then why does it seem so impossible? To begin, it's helpful to realize that "impossible" doesn't exist on some grand cosmic level. *It's only impossible for us because we've never done it before.*

The mission of creating the change we want is impossible for who we are *used to* being and what we're *used to* doing, thinking, and believing. Our dreams and passionate ideas haven't come true because our lives aren't organized around making them happen. Instead, they're organized around *not* making our dreams happen. We're not yet in the right energetic shape to do what it will take to create the change we want.

"Energetic shape" is shorthand for all the ways we habitually shape our lives – psychologically, physically, emotionally, in our relationships, and in all our other habits and ways of going about life. We don't have the lives we want, we haven't reinvented ourselves and seen our Big Ideas come to fruition, because we haven't restructured ourselves and our ways of going about life in a way that will make them happen.

To get something new, *we need to become something new.* And that means changing *everything* in us and in our lives that doesn't support the new thing.

Whoa. That's intense. Did you say *everything?*

Yes.

No wonder we blanche when inspiration comes calling. Remake everything? Who's going to take a deal on those kinds of terms?

We are, if we really want something new.

WANT CHANGE?
TRANSFORMATION 101

(Part 3 of 3)

"Self-awareness is the gentle motivator for change," a friend of mine used to say.

Maybe so, but who's got time for that? Take time for "Know thyself"? Sorry, I've got something going on that night.

Socrates said "The unexamined life is not worth living." Good advice which most of us don't follow. But self-awareness isn't optional when we're after our dreams. Which is why, once we decide to set our dreams free from where we've been hiding them, it's all about us, all the time.

No, that's not an accusation from a relationship gone bad. It's what happens when we dare to answer inspiration's call to create change in our lives. The bigger the change we want, the more we can't just change *things*. Big change means we have to change *ourselves* as well. And that's not going to happen without a big dose of self-awareness. Our unexamined life is about to become examined. Big time.

Self-awareness goes digging, roots out those pockets of resistance. It tells us when we're trying to get the new by using the old, when we're believing one thing while trying to do another, when we're trying to get there by being reasonable. And lots more. Gotta have it.

There are lots of paths to self-awareness. Choose one. And forget the shortcuts – there aren't any, and besides this is too important.

Personal transformation is not just a good idea for the enlightened, consciousness-raising few, it's essential to achieving every person's Big Idea. We cannot achieve the change we want, cannot create the lives or the world we want, without changing ourselves first.

We aren't prepared for this. We think we can just shift what we've always been and done – what we've believed, what we've known, how we've made decisions and how we've acted, all our customary tools and habits – to our new project.

We're wrong. We and the new thing we want are created together, or not at all.

WHERE CHANGE BEGINS: INSPIRATION

(Part 1 of 3)

C hange starts with inspiration. Inspiration ignites us. It is both fuel and fire, the match that strikes and the blaze that bursts. Inspiration makes the impossible possible. Without inspiration, we'd never change or create anything.

At the core of inspiration is this one idea: *something else is possible...and because it is, everything must move aside to make room for it.* No, more than that – everything else must become new.

Inspiration invades our numbed lives, overwhelms our defenses. It disconnects our habitual sense of what is normal and possible, detaches our allegiances to status quo. One minute we have an ironclad case for The Way Things Are; the next we're tearing it down. One minute we're drifting and purposeless; the next we have a cause to throw down for.

Inspiration is our beginning. It is also our destination – the shining new reality we will inhabit when our idea unites with our hope and takes shape in our lives. What we see and think and feel when inspiration greets us is what we'll see and think and feel on that grand and glorious day when we finally arrive where inspiration calls us to go.

Sometimes, inspiration comes with visions of glory. When it does, it thrills us with new passions and possibilities, shocks our unused neural pathways into unaccustomed life. It shakes us awake in the dead of night, urges us to our feet and outside to gaze into deep space. It plays a new tune on a new instrument, until our long submerged essence resonates with a new boldness, stunned at the robustness of its own long-silenced voice.

Inspiration awakens us to glory days we live with abandon. We revel in their freedom, joy, and passion. They are the days of newness and discovery, celebration and vigor – the days of wildness and courage and daring, the sweeping dive of new love, the dizzy freshness of everything that's good about life.

At other times, inspiration isn't so kind or so pretty.

WHERE CHANGE BEGINS:
WAKE UP CALL

(Part 2 of 3)

Aformer Marine drill sergeant once told me how they "greeted" new recruits – stomping into their barracks at 3:00 a.m., shouting and cracking whips. "I guess you could say we gave them a wake up call," he chuckled. Then he got serious. "They needed to know right away that they weren't in Kansas anymore. Otherwise they weren't going to survive boot camp, let alone the kind of combat we send them into."

Wake up calls jolt us into a present, unpleasant reality. They leave us disoriented, lost, afraid. They create tension, discomfort, dissonance. They ask us to take an unflinching look at what's uncomfortable in our world – what's making us unhappy, what we'd like to change. And not just what's in our world, but what's in *us*.

Lots of people have gotten nasty wake up calls the past few years: the tough economy, job loss, business failure, downsizing, foreclosure, bankruptcy. Sometimes wake up calls aren't so harsh, but come more subtly, from inside – a restless longing to pursue a dream, a resolve to reinvent ourselves in midlife, or a vague sense that all is not well in our world.

How wake up calls come to us ultimately isn't important. What's important is how we deal with them. It takes courage to wake up. It takes more courage to *stay* awake, and get moving in the direction of the change we want to see. There are always an overwhelming number of good reasons not to change – which is why most of use go right on living our lives of quiet desperation.

And to make it worse, our dreams just won't leave us alone. They keep coming back – a nudge, an invitation, a crazy idea. Each time is more forceful than the last. If we keep putting them off, next time the wake up call might come drill sergeant style.

Just be warned, that's all.

WHERE CHANGE BEGINS:
IMPOSSIBLE MISSION,
UNLIKELY HERO

(Part 3 of 3)

W hy does its seem like our grandest visions bother to come to us when they could've found someone a whole lot better qualified? Inspiration does that to you. It surprises you, lays the whole glorious vision out there in high def, then drops the impossible mission on you, knowing full well there's no possible way you could ever do it. And then it asks whether you'll accept your mission anyway.

A few years back, I launched out to pursue a big dream of producing a stage spectacle. People were encouraging – they told me it wasn't completely outlandish to think I could do it. I was a lawyer with a creative streak. So what? There are lots of those around. Surely the combination of right-brained aptitude and left-brained education and experience would help me out. Right?

I appreciated their support, but knew better. A career of advising small business owners wasn't going to help with a multi-million dollar business plan or its capital requirements. Running a law firm of five lawyers and support staff hadn't done anything to prepare me for managing a cast and crew and other independent service providers and product vendors totaling over 70. Diddling around in theater hadn't taught me the artistic and technical intricacies of putting on a multimedia stage spectacle. And on it went. There was no way I could justify to myself that I was the man for the job.

How did I deal with my lack of qualification? In the end, I didn't. I didn't pursue my Big Idea because I *could*, I did it because when no one else wanted the job, it was up to me or I was going to have to let the whole crazy idea go. And I couldn't, I just couldn't. It had its hooks in me too deeply. So I accepted the impossible mission.

That's what we do when inspiration gets its hooks in us. There will be all sorts of sound and well-educated reasons for NOT doing the thing we feel inspired to do, but in the end none of them can explain that initial moment of inspiration when we see and hear and feel that thing that moves our hearts so much we just *have* to give it a try.

If that's not a calling, it'll do until the real thing comes along.

LIFE IN THE GAP

Part 1: **How to Get Over an Inspirational Hangover
(Or, Why New Year's Resolutions Don't Work)**

At the gym where I used to work out, the regulars used to gather this time of year to complain about how crowded the place was with all the "The Resolutioners." But don't worry, they'd say smugly, they'll all be gone by mid-February. And they were right, year after year.

New Year's Resolutions rarely work. Why not?

We make them because we've had some time off, got relaxed, found ourselves reflecting about the things in our life that chronically make us dissatisfied. We tell ourselves this time we're going to do something about it – get healthier, change jobs, start a company, take up a new hobby, whatever. Maybe we even dare to share our new thoughts and plans with someone else.

And then we wake up with an inspirational hangover. What were we thinking? Inspiration flew the coop overnight, taking all those new thoughts and ideas with it, and we're left hoping we didn't do anything too stupid while we were under the influence.

We mean well. We start well. We don't finish well. Why not?

Because we're not prepared for the ferocity of the Resistance with a capital R we run into when we try to change things in our lives. Everybody who's ever tried to make good on a New Year's Resolution knows about Resistance. It always shows up, never misses its cue, and it's always pissed off. And it always brings the same message: What were you thinking? Don't you realize you're making a fool of yourself? We wither under its barrage, go limping back to status quo.

Resistance is a fact of life in the world of change, and there's no use trying something new without knowing how to deal with it. The good news is, we can learn, and when we do, we get to be one of those smug regulars the next time January rolls around.

The first thing we need to learn about is life in the Gap.

LIFE IN THE GAP

Part 2: **Take a Facer** *(Not a bow)*

We got inspired, we went for it. So now what? Time to take a bow while the world applauds our resolution? Nope. The bows will have to wait. What comes first isn't a bow, it's a facer... into the Gap.

The Gap is Resistance with a capital R. It's the distance between what we have now and what we want to have when our dreams come true. If we want our Big Ideas to come to fruition, we must live through the Gap, because that's where we're equipped to meet the challenges we need to meet and make the changes we need to make in order to finally prevail.

It's not so bad at first, when we're still freshly charged with inspiration. Meeting challenges is fun. We find resourcefulness we didn't know we had. There's a sense of triumph in overcoming. But after awhile the challenges get tougher, and it's not so fun anymore.

Change is tough; there are a thousand reasons to quit, and sooner or later one of them is too alluring to resist. Sooner or later we hit one too many obstacles, become overwhelmed and afraid, bail out and scurry back to the safety of whatever we left, leaving our half-executed plans and unrealized visions strewn behind us.

That's life in the Gap. No wonder people give up on their dreams.

Life in the Gap is about hitting barriers, and hitting them hard. A friend of mine calls this "crash dummy syndrome": you hit so many brick walls that after awhile when you hit a new one it's not a catastrophe, it's just another day at the office. Brick wall incoming! BAM! Go back and do it again. BAM! Do it again. BAM!

Crash dummies save lives. In the Gap, we're the crash dummies. Is that any way to live?

It is when the life you're saving is your own.

Once we're in the Gap, the only way *out* is *through*. And to get through, we must overcome not only the Gap's *challenges*, we must also overcome *ourselves*.

LIFE IN THE GAP

Part 3: **Hell Hath No Fury Like an Ego Scorned**

What we're up against in the Gap is "ego." By that, I mean what makes us who we are – the dynamic organizing principle that gives our lives psychic shape and physical expression, that creates and sustains who we are, what we do, and what we have.

Ego accounts for how we make decisions, our likes and dislikes, our areas of competence and ignorance. It draws reality into orbit around itself, defines what's normal and what's not, what's safe and possible and predictable, and what isn't.

Ego was formed when we were young, to make us feel safe in a scary world. It gives us our sense of self, creates boundaries that differentiate us from others. It's the summation of the beliefs and behaviors that shapes our habitual experience of life.

Ego is why we resist change – *even the change we want.* Ego blocks new ideas not on their merits but as a matter of policy, because it has created – on a deep, subconscious level we're probably not in touch with – beliefs that some things are possible for ourselves and some things aren't. When we challenge those beliefs, they resist us, and until we root them out, they're going to prevent us.

The Gap comes into existence when we dare to defy those beliefs by moving toward what we want. The Resistance we meet in the Gap is ego shuddering in the face of our passionate commitment to change. The bigger the change, the greater the threat, and the fiercer ego's resistance. Ego began as a normal part of psychological and social development when we were kids. Now it turns on us. What was once our friend and teacher and bodyguard is now our Resistance.

Ego can't create the new, but it can and will sabotage our efforts to do so. Either we break ego's control over us or we go back where we came. The Gap is where we settle the issue.

And hell hath no fury like an ego scorned.

LIFE IN THE GAP

Part 4: **Things Could Get a Little Bouncy Up Ahead**

The Gap is a violent clash of energies – turbulence to the nth degree.

On the one hand, there's the energy of what we want: visionary. idealistic, imaginative. It puts a gleam in our inspired eye, fills us with passion, makes us reach for the stars. It's fun to think about the new possibilities. We feel determined, purposeful.

On the other hand, there's the energy of The Way Things Are – reasonable, established, entrenched. It doesn't see what we see when we're all inspired, and it doesn't care anyway. All it knows is that there's a right and wrong way to do things, and what we have in mind is definitely the wrong way. Sit down before you hurt yourself. You're rocking the boat.

Throw those two energies together, and they're like the Capulets and the Montagues crossing paths in the marketplace. There's gonna be trouble.

What's worse, the Gap is our handiwork. We hit turbulence when we take off in the pursuit of our big ideas. We *cause* it. As long as we're moving ahead with our plans to create something new, it might get a little bouncy up ahead. (Don't you love it when the pilot comes on the intercom and says that?)

When we move in the direction of accomplishing something new, we stress our relationships, our routines, our habitual ways of thinking and believing and doing things. We *have* to, because if we don't, nothing's going to change. That's why, whenever we chase a new dream or goal or big idea, we also chase storms. No, more than that – we *create* storms. And the bigger the change we want, the more violent the storm is going to be. A little bouncy? When it comes to the Gap, it's more like *Storm-Chaser.*

We can stop anytime, and it won't be turbulent anymore. But making things calm down comes at a stiff price: we need to stop moving toward the goals we want to achieve, the new thing we want to create. Do we really want that? Of course not. We set out to change things. Giving up is a shortcut back to status quo. Been there, done that.

So if we're on the path to change, we need to buckle up. It could get a little bouncy up ahead.

FULL ACCOUNTABILITY

(Part 1)

C hange of any kind – a new strategic direction for the firm, pursuing a personal dream, reinventing ourselves after a job layoff, achieving a personal or business "stretch" goal – starts with a simple belief that the change we want is possible. Stake ourselves on a belief like that, and the doubts invariably come. Can we *really* get free of status quo and create something new in its place?

Believe it or not, the answer is always positive. Not only *can* we, we already do. We *already* have *exactly* what we want. Right now. We created it.

No way.

Yes way. *What we've already got is what we want.* Or at least what we *wanted.* Our current circumstances reveal our past desires and beliefs, the choices we've made and how we've acted. They tell us what's gone before, what got us to this moment.

We did all that. We are responsible for getting ourselves to where we are, right here and now. We created THE WAY THINGS ARE. If we want to continue accepting it as status quo going forward, we can. But we don't have to. We have a choice. We can choose to create something new, just the same way we created our current reality.

A friend explained this to me over coffee one day, and it didn't sit well. I wanted to niggle about loopholes and exceptions. But then I thought, why would I want to? So what if I can find holes in this theory – what's that going to get me? Wouldn't I rather take responsibility for believing and behaving in ways that further my goals? If that's what it takes to produce what I want, then why wouldn't I embrace this way of thinking?

Besides, debate is pointless anyway, because full accountability doesn't ask us to believe we can control *everything*. It only asks us to believe that *we* are in control of what we *believe* and how we *behave*, and that those things create our lives.

If we created what we no longer want, we can use the same creative power to do the opposite. That's the principle of full accountability. Ready to give it a shot?

FULL ACCOUNTABILITY

(Part 2)

Full accountability is one of those new thoughts that make our brains hurt because they travel over previously unused neural pathways. New thoughts like that are uncomfortable and awkward, but we get used to them with practice. Besides, to move in the direction of our goals and dreams, we don't have to win a debate with our old way of thinking. We just need to be willing to move ourselves ahead by trying out new ways of thinking, and full accountability is one of them.

Then why wouldn't we do that?

Well, for one thing, we all know that there are true victims in life, and we can set that up as an excuse. But we're not talking about those kinds of victims here. We're talking about you and me, wanting to make some changes. If we use the "I'm not in control of everything" argument to justify our own inaction, then it easily becomes one big all-powerful excuse to justify all the rest of our *other* excuses – the justification of all justifications for self-imposed victimhood. No thanks. Been there, done that. Time for something new.

And for another thing, once we start practicing full accountability, we can't get away with squat. We used to be able to go mindlessly along, creating lives we didn't want and blaming Fate or dumb luck or other people or whatever. No more. Now, when we ask why our dreams and big ideas and plans aren't happening, the finger points back at us, and the only issue is whether we'd like the long or short version.

The short one will do, if we're willing to act on it.

Besides, if we accept that we created the things in our lives that we now want to change, that means we have the power to create new things to replace them. That's what we get when we embrace the principle of full accountability: we get the power to change. We're not victims anymore. We can *do* this.

You hear people talk about not giving away our power. To think and act contrary to the principle of full accountability is to give away our power to change. That kind of victimhood is voluntary. Most of us learned long ago to never volunteer. How come we volunteer so eagerly for *that?*

THE FAILURE CHRONICLES:
LEARNING TO LIVE WITH FAILURE

Part 1 of 3

I recently watched a TED talk by Regina Dugan, the director of DARPA (the Defense Advanced Research Projects Agency). She leads a group of people whose job, simply put, is to do the impossible. They work on things like creating airplanes that can fly at Mach 20, which would get you coast-to-coast in less than 12 minutes. Their longest flight to date has been about 3 minutes. After that, the thing keeps burning up.

She challenged us with that question we've all heard so many times we've become hardened to it: "What would you attempt to do if you knew you could not fail?" If we can get over our cynicism for a moment, we'll find it's a useful question, because it brings our fear of failure front and center where we can deal with it.

"Failure is part of creating," Ms. Dugan said. "We cannot fear failure and create new and amazing things." She quoted Georges Clemenceau: "Life gets interesting if you fail, because it means we've surpassed ourselves."

"We've surpassed ourselves." Yes. We haven't overcome external obstacles, we've challenged the barriers inside of us, such as how we think and what we believe. To do the impossible, we have to believe that maybe it – whatever the "it" in question might be - isn't impossible after all. Why is believing that so hard for us? Because we're afraid to fail.

What if we refuse to think that way? What if instead we follow DARPA's example? They can't believe in failure, otherwise they'd never get anything done. No, check that, they'd never get anything *started*. They must accept failure as an essential part of their work. That's the only way they can find out for themselves what truly is and isn't "impossible."

Which is why they can create things like a mechanical surveillance hummingbird that weighs less than a AA battery and is equipped with a camera. ("The world's first hummingbird pilot" flew it onstage during Ms. Dugan's talk.)

Walt Disney said, "It's kind of fun to do the impossible." He also said, You may not realize it when it happens, but a kick in the teeth may be the best thing in the world for you." I guess he, too, knew something about dealing with failure.

THE FAILURE CHRONICLES: WHAT IF THERE WERE NO SUCH THING AS FAILURE?

(Part 2 of 3)

I f we don't achieve what we want, that means we failed, right? Wrong. That's only true if we believe in failure. I personally don't.

What?!

Hear me out, but first think about this: "You're a failure!" is one of the meanest judgments we can pronounce. Most of us are much too kind to say that to someone else, but we'll say it to ourselves. Why? And why aren't we *overjoyed* to hear that maybe we've been wrong all this time, that failure actually doesn't exist?

Maybe it's because we're used to holding onto failure as the ultimate consolation booby prize. We do that because somewhere deep inside we believe we really can't have and do and be what we want. That dismal belief comes from the same root that causes us to value pain, struggle, hardship, lack, need, impossibility, insurmountable barriers, striving, denial, endless back-breaking, soul-killing, fruitless labor, powerlessness, unrequited sacrifice, and pointless self-martyr-hood. That root belief is a noxious weed. Let's pull it out.

I don't believe in failure because I don't buy that it's a state of *fact* we have to accept. Instead, I think it's a *judgment – a state of mind that's optional, something we don't have to believe it we don't want to.* We create the "fact" of failure by pronouncing the *judgment* of failure. If we refuse to make that judgment, then failure doesn't exist. The thing we used to call failure is now just an accepted part of the creative process.

Learning to think that way is a mental garden we need to cultivate. We start by planting the seed of the possibility that failure, however perversely satisfying to the fearful voice of status quo, may not in fact be as good or desirable as success, for the same reason that struggle may not be as good as ease, deprivation may not be as good as plenty, isolation may not be as good as connection, and remaining dull may not be as good as being awake.

If I can never fail, then I'll never be a failure. What a relief! Instead, I can be one of those creative people who always seems to think the triumphant finale is just one more plot twist away, so they keep going just to find out.

Where's the failure in that? It's all in our heads, that's where

THE FAILURE CHRONICLES:
GIVING UP ON QUITTING

(Part 3 of 3)

Whenever we get deep into something we judge as not going well, we start to panic. "Quit while you can," the voice of fear says, "because the odds are getting worse by the minute. You're going to fail, you're going to fail, you're going to fail...."

That's a lie. Bookmakers set odds beforehand. The odds don't change once the game is on. Besides, we're playing to win, no matter what the odds.

It's a good thing that sometimes those fearful warnings fall on deaf ears. Otherwise we'd never get to make heroes out of people who persevered and triumphed even though everyone told them to give up. We love those stories, and ours could be one of them. How about we think about *that* the next time we're inclined to pronounce a failure judgment on ourselves?

With some practice, we'll start to believe we can actually give up on failure. Which means we can also give up on quitting, too. If we can't fail, then why quit? It took guts to get started, and it took more to keep going, so why stop now? The story's just getting good!

Besides, hedging bets is for professional investors and gamblers, not for people trying to make their dreams and visions and big ideas a reality.

We reach for the word failure when we get to the point where we want to scream to anyone who will listen that we've given it our all and the whole thing isn't working so why bother anymore. But the truth is, no we haven't. Determination defies endurance. Just because we're broke, lonely, worn out, and discouraged doesn't mean we've got nothing left. There's always more.

Maybe we cling to the possibly of failure because that lets us hold a little something in reserve when we try to do the impossible. That strategy appeals to our fearful side, but ironically and perversely, the thing we're holding back might be the difference between getting or not getting what we want.

Besides, what are we holding it back for anyway? So we can keep open the opportunity to return to whatever we wanted to leave behind in the first place?

No thanks. Life is tricky enough without taking on its challenges with one hand tied behind our back. I say we give up on failure instead. And while we're at it, let's give up on quitting, too.

RUNNING PAST OUR LIMITS (2012)

Part 1: Onto Something Big

At my workshops, I sometimes I get asked to tell my story. I usually don't. I think it implies that my story is somehow more valuable than anybody else's. We're all in this make-your-dreams-come-true thing together, and I want to keep it that way.

But this time I'm going to make an exception, because I've stumbled onto something so big and amazing there's no way anybody could think it's just about me. It's huge, and if all of us could tap into this, we and our lives and our world would change – maybe as fast as overnight. Really, It's that good. Here's the story:

For reasons I won't bore you with (okay, I've had a couple accidents, that's all you get for now), I have trouble walking. Running is impossible. You name it, I've tried it: rehab, PT, lifting, stretching, massage, acupuncture, chiropractic, energy therapy... No luck so far. But I love to work out, and last September (2011) my daughter was home and wanted to lose some weight she'd put on during a year in France. (*Bon appétit!*) So she'd go to Bally Total Fitness with me and get on the elliptical machine, and I'd get on the one next to her. She'd go maybe an hour. I'd go maybe 10 minutes.

She lost the weight she wanted to lose, and I got an idea: "I wonder if I could start running on this machine, the way I used to before I got hurt?" I also wondered if maybe somewhere along the way my body would decide to start working again like it did before.

Then I got a second, totally crazy, wild hare idea. "I wonder if I could do 12 miles in 60 minutes on this thing?" Never mind that I have trouble walking to the end of the block. I have no idea where the idea came from; it just did. But I do know that twelve 5-minute miles is fast.

So I started in, grinding out maybe a mile in 12 or 15 minutes. My ankles and feet don't have much feeling in them, and when I walk my hips and legs sort of stop working, so that I have to drag myself along. I call it my Quasimodo walk. And so when I was done with my elliptical sessions I could barely get off the machine. I'd look around, trying to make sure nobody noticed as I staggered and wobbled over to a chair. I'd collect myself and then go staggering and wobbling home (I have a cane, but hate to use it), afraid some cop was going to come by and stop me for public drunkenness. (Seriously.)

I worked on pace and stamina throughout the fall, and discovered something *really important*: when my feet and ankles are numb and my legs stop working, I can still make the elliptical move. I don't have to actually pick up my feet (which is a problem), all I have to do is *glide*. (Hint: That's important. Remember that for later.)

RUNNING PAST OUR LIMITS (2012)

Part 2: Don't Call the Ambulance

I started to get faster and go further. About the time winter was arriving, I did 5 miles in 66 minutes, then at Christmas I did 7 in 82. One day I decided to go as long as I could, which turned out to be an hour and 45 minutes. I don't remember how far I went. When I got home, my wife was frantic. I'd been gone so long, she thought the people at Bally Total Fitness must have sent me off in an ambulance.

One day when I was feeling really strong I decided to try to run a 5 minute mile, just to see if it was physically possible. The machine shook and wobbled - apparently I was pushing the limits of more than just me. I labored, but I did it. So now I knew it was theoretically possible to run 12 miles in an hour.

Around Christmas two terrific things happened. One day I was gliding along with my eyes shut, as I often did, when a pat on the back made me jump. It was our local Bally amazon. "Working hard!" was all she said. A couple weeks later I was limping toward the door after a workout ("Just limp," my wife had advised, "You don't look drunk that way."), when a guy my age met my eyes. "Man, you work out hard," he said. "Yes, I do," I replied.

You can go a long way on encouragement like that.

What about my goal of 12 miles in 60 minutes? Um, not so much. Yes, it was theoretically possible, and I'd made great progress on both pace and distance, but that goal was shooting at the moon. Around mid-January, I gave up on it. There were still too many days when my legs just wouldn't move anymore and I'd have to quit after a mile or so and go trudging home in despair.

Plus, as a healing modality, this hadn't been my best idea. My feet and legs were getting worse, not better, although it was hard to tell if that was because of my new exercise regime or not – they've been getting worse for awhile. But despite that, I was *feeling* better – inside at least. My heart and lungs had to be loving it – especially my heart, in more ways than one. So I kept on.

And then one day, maybe a month or two after I gave up on my goal, I got a new idea – another totally crazy, wild hare idea: "I wonder if I could run a marathon on this thing?"

RUNNING PAST OUR LIMITS:

Part 3: Meet Coach

A curious thing started to happen as I entertained the idea of running a marathon on the elliptical: I got a coach. Well, I already had one for other things, but now he got involved with my running program.

I don't think I've told you about Coach before, have I? In short, he's that part of me that accepts what I say I want at face value, and never doubts that I truly want it or can achieve it. He's that drive inside me that *will not accept that something is impossible* if I really, really want it, that believes in me no matter what, and won't let me quit or call myself a failure.

It's nice to have a guy like that around - not that I wouldn't like to strangle him sometimes. He's a disciplinarian, but always fair and never cruel. He's also frequently exasperating, because he never knows when to call it quits, never recognizes when I've reached my absolute, all-out limit. He always thinks I've got more to give, and always requires it of me.

Maybe you'd like to meet him. You can. He's imaginary, but that doesn't mean he's not real. I'm convinced you've got a coach like mine inside of you. Yours will look and act differently than mine, but he or she will do the same things for you that mine does for me. You might want to go looking inside yourself to see if you can find one and get acquainted.

Anyway, once I started to think about doing a marathon, Coach started showing up for my workouts. I'd finish a session on the machine and sit down to recover, and then I'd hear a voice in my head. "Think you could do another mile?" Or, "Think you could do three more miles at 8 minutes?" Or whatever.

Usually, the questions came at a point in my workout when the answer was an emphatic, "No!" And then he'd say, "Think you could do it anyway?" And so I would, and I'd hit whatever the workout goal was, usually right on the nose. It was uncanny.

With Coach's help, my pace and stamina went leaping forward. My wife quit worrying about how long I was gone at my workouts. Along the way, I taught myself some quick recovery techniques – breathing, stretching – that shortened my break times.

I also started visualizing. You hear about athletes doing that. If nothing else, it's a good way to pass the time when you're on an elliptical for an hour – a whole lot better than watching the energy-sucking crap on all the TV's. I'd see myself running a marathon, being the shocking old white dude who could keep up with those guys from Kenya and Ethiopia who can run impossibly far impossibly fast.

I became an international marathon phenom. It was fun, and I always won every race.

RUNNING PAST OUR LIMITS (2012)

Part 4: Race Day

Winter became spring, and I didn't have a date for my marathon, but when I started running 12, then 15, then 18 miles, I knew it must be getting close. I *did* have a time goal: three hours. That's just under seven minutes per mile. From what I can tell, three hours is a dividing line for marathoners, the level where you're starting to get serious. One day I ran 8 miles at that pace, took a break and ran 7 more. "You could run all day at that pace," I heard Coach say, and I knew he was right.

Coach had started showing up not *during* my workouts, like he used to, but on the way over to Bally. We'd discuss goals and plans for the day, and I'd almost always hit them on the nose, no matter how aggressive they were. There were still days when I had to quit early, but fewer.

I thought I might do my marathon the same weekend as the Colfax Marathon in May, so I looked up last year's winning time for someone my age, and it was just under 3 hours. Right on target. But then on the last Sunday in April I woke up, and I just knew. Today was the day. I didn't tell my wife when I left for Bally. I was afraid to jinx it, I guess.

I did the first 10 miles faster than my target pace, but when they were over I had lost all feeling in my ankles and feet. I had to stop to stretch and massage and fill up my water bottle. I wanted to do the next 8 miles in a single stretch, but had to stop halfway for more water and more stretching and massaging. The bottom half of my legs were swollen, one of my hamstrings kept cramping, and the places where I had some fractures were aching. It didn't look good.

I finished the first 18 and sat for awhile, kicking my feet and trying to get the feeling back, wondering if I was done. And then there was Coach's gentle voice. "Think you could get back on and go a little further?" My answer was "No!" And then I got back on.

I'd hit the infamous Wall that marathoners talk about. I lasted the next 2½ miles on sheer guts, got off and staggered over to sit down. No way. Again the voice. "Think you could go further?" I did a mile and a half, and got off again. I was done. It was over. I had no feeling below my knees, my ankles and calves looked like Elephant Man. Again the voice. I did another 1.2 miles, at one point looking down at the read-out on the machine to see that I hadn't lost that much pace. Amazingly, my three hour goal was still possible. Too bad finishing wasn't.

It didn't matter that Coach insists on believing that whatever I want to do is possible. He was wrong this time. Impossible obviously had won. I was 23.2 miles into a marathon, and no matter how many times Coach asked me to keep going, it wasn't going to happen. Even if I could've found the will, finishing was physically impossible. My body was in full rebellion. It wasn't going anywhere.

I sat there in total defeat, and all I could think was, "I'm 3 miles from the finish line! I just can't quit now!" In a fog of defeat, I got up and dragged myself back to the machine. I picked up my first leg with both hands and put it on one of the pedals, then dragged the second foot up.

RUNNING PAST OUR LIMITS (2012)

Part 5: "I'm So Proud of You!"

Three miles to go. I glided along, keeping my eyes on the distance and pace read-outs on the machine. It felt like running through a swamp, but I kept telling myself to just glide, just keep gliding. And amazingly, I was still on pace. I closed my eyes and visualized crowds of people lining the streets, chanting, waving, cheering. I opened my eyes after a bit, and saw two things that made me mentally stagger.

The first was that I'd run another mile. The second was my wife, standing there. She'd been off walking, enjoying the park that morning. She'd taken a nap in the sun, and when she woke up, she knew. She knew I was running the race I hadn't dared to tell her about, because I'd been afraid I might fail. And she knew she had to be there at the finish line.

She dashed over to Bally and told the guys at the front desk that no, I'm not a member, but that's my husband over there and he's running a marathon and I need to be there when he finishes.

I don't think I've ever seen a more welcome sight. She met my eyes when I opened them. "I'm so proud of you," she said. She started to cry. I started to cry. Ever try to finish a marathon when you're crying? My tears poured down my face with my sweat, which was already burning in my eyes. "And Coach is going nuts," she added.

You gotta understand: Coach is as buttoned up as they come. He's a Tom Landry lookalike: suit, tie, London Fog topcoat, felt fedora, the whole works. I closed my eyes, and there at the edge of the crowd was Coach, waving his sport coat over his head and whooping it up. It was too much, it made me start to cry again, so I opened my eyes.

"I'm so proud of you!" my wife said again. "You can do it!" I sent her off to get some water or paper towels or something. I didn't really want her to leave, but I had to quit crying and focus on finishing. The last mile was my fastest of the day. I burst under the arch of balloons as the crowd roared and Janet cried and Coach whooped.

And then it was over. I dropped off the machine and stood, unable to move. My time was 2:51:57. That's counting only the time I spent actually moving on the machine, not the time I spent trying to get feeling back in my feet and all the rest. If I'd counted all that, it probably would have added another 20-25 minutes. I decided to cut myself some slack and not count the extra.

"I just ran a marathon on the elliptical," I told the guys at the front desk as I left. They didn't seem all that impressed. Oh well, I didn't do it for them.

I have two more running exploits to tell you about, and then I'll draw some conclusions, and this series of blog posts will be over.

RUNNING PAST OUR LIMITS:

Part 6: Gliding Into the New Normal

A week later, I ran another marathon. I didn't plan to do it. I just woke up in a mood, checked in with Coach, got the nod, and did it. My time was 2:35:58 – 16 minutes faster than the week before. I missed the world record for a man my age by a minute and 35 seconds. Even if I had counted the time off the machine, refilling my water bottle and working to get the feeling back in my feet, I still would have come in under the original 3 hour goal I'd had for the week before.

Funny, the first time, when I shared my marathon story with family and friends, everybody got all inspired. This time, it was no big deal. Oh, Kevin/Dad ran another marathon. I wonder what's for dinner.

A couple weeks later, I hit my goal of 12 miles in 60 minutes – the goal I'd set eight months ago and given up on four months later. Again, when I woke up that day, I just knew it was time. I checked in with Coach, and he was good with it. When I finished, I plopped down on the bench in the locker room, drenched in sweat, internally celebrating. I took off my shoes, and then... there was Coach's gentle voice. "Think you could do five more?"

By now, I've learned that Coach only asks me to do what he knows I can do, even if I don't agree. We set a pace goal of 5:15 for the five miles. It was tough going, and I did them at 5:35 –it was the first time in a long time I hadn't hit a goal, but it was still worth feeling good about. Again I headed to the locker room, and when I reached for the combination lock on my locker, the voice came again. "Think you could do two more?" I didn't bother to spin the lock. "I'll do three," I said, and headed back out. My pace was 5:20.

I want to do my next elliptical machine marathon in 2:20:00. That's a 5:20 pace. It will beat the world record for my age by 14 minutes. Then I want to run one as fast as those guys from Africa. That will be a 4:40 pace. And I want to celebrate my 60th birthday by running a *real* marathon under 3 hours.

No, I don't actually run. All I have to do is glide. And no, I don't count the time when I have to get off the machine to get water and tend to my physical limitations, which haven't gotten any better – not yet, anyway.

So what do we learn from all this? You've long since figured out that this series of blog posts isn't about running marathons on the elliptical machine. Instead, it's about running past our limits, whatever they are. It's about doing things we *know* are impossible. Apparently we can live in two realities at once. In one, there is no possible way we can do the thing we want. In the other reality, we can, and the first reality's negative opinion doesn't count. The first time we do it, we're stunned and astonished, and so is everyone else. The second time, it's just routine. What used to be impossible has now become the new normal.

What's the new normal you'd like to create for yourself? Like I said back at the start, if all of us could tap into this idea of doing the impossible, we and our lives and our world would change, maybe overnight.

And all we have to do is just keep gliding along.

CHANGE WITHOUT JUDGMENT

(Part 1)

We often initiate change from a place of deficiency. I'm out of shape; I need to go on a diet. I'm unhappy at work; I need to find a new career. I lost my job; I need to find a new one.

We probably had some kind of wakeup call, and we're alarmed enough to get into crisis mode and change some things. When we make change that way, it's like we're confessing that we broke some kind of law or moral or ethical code: I *shouldn't* be out of shape or unsuccessful or unhappy or out of a job – those things are *wrong*. We're motivated by guilt or unhappiness or other similar emotion.

That's a common and normal motivation for change. It's also rarely effective over the long haul.

Why not? Because when we approach change this way, we actually unleash two competing energies: one seeks change, and the other promises to punish us if we don't succeed. This results in a state of internal dissonance, which is what happens when we hold competing beliefs about something. In time, the prospect of punishment and accompanying feelings of fear and guilt and shame overwhelm our good intentions. Our souls are like a stringed instrument with two strings just off, vibrating in that way that makes the oscilloscope bounce all over the place.

That state of clashing energy won't sustain us in the long term. Deterrence maybe works in the criminal code, but it's rarely good for our souls. We're better off changing from a place of internal harmony. I know that sounds touchy-feely, but don't worry, we aren't going to hold hands and sing Kumbayah. We just need to learn to make change from a place of being internally in tune.

Trying to make change under the glowering specter of judgment doesn't promote harmony. If we don't move past the initial shock of the wakeup call and get to a more sustainable internal place, then achieving the change we want is going to be a tough slog of one step forward, two steps back. Sucking it up and gutting it out can get us a long way, but it won't get us all the way home.

How about we try something different? How about we try the kind of change that comes when our souls get on the same frequency as our dreams and plans and intentions? How about we make changes by responding to a genuine internal urge to be and do and have what we want?

We can do that by practicing Change Without Judgment. Let's find out how.

CHANGE WITHOUT JUDGMENT

(Part 2)
Getting Over the Threshold

I n his book *The Writer's Journey*, Christopher Vogler says this about "threshold guardians."

> But on a deeper level they [threshold guardians] stand for our internal demons: the neuroses, emotional scars, vices, dependencies, and self-limitations that hold back our growth and progress. It seems that every time you try to make a major change in your life, these inner demons rise up to their full force, not necessarily to stop you, but to test if you're really determined to accept the challenge of change.

Threshold guardians are the guards and gatekeepers who stand in the hero's way, usually early in the journey. You know all about them if you've ever tried to make a big change in your life. You start to change and immediately find yourself nose-to-nose with the same old fears and limiting beliefs that have always held you back.

What do we usually do when that happens? We lapse into the same old defeatist thinking that kept us from changing before. What if I fail? What will they think? (Whoever *they* are!) Who do I think I am, that I should want this? And all the rest.

All that is part of making big change. But we don't see it that way. Instead, we *judge ourselves* for running into these gatekeepers, for having these demons in our psyches. Look at me! I'm so bad! I'm such a failure! I'll never make it! And so on.

We need to get past our threshold guardians if we want to move on. We do that by first recognizing that they aren't external. They come from within; they're the things we create in our own psyches that stand in our way of being and doing something different. Because they're internal, they're the toughest barriers to get over. We know how to overcome external challenges; it's much harder to get over ourselves. And one thing is for sure: blaming ourselves and feeling defeated isn't going to help.

What is going to help? Vogler's book offers us a clue:

Successful heroes learn to recognize Threshold Guardians not as threatening enemies but as useful Allies and early indicators that new power or success is coming.

That's right: our biggest challenges are usually our best opportunities. Instead of beating ourselves up for them, we can learn to welcome and celebrate them. No kidding!

Sometimes, all our internal gatekeepers want before they'll let us pass is as simple as (a) gratitude plus (b) resolve to keep moving anyway. An attitude of "Wow, look at me – I'm making progress!" instead of "I must be doing something wrong" makes all the difference

CHANGE WITHOUT JUDGMENT

(Part 3)
Wanting What We Want

Most of us are afraid to want what we want. What's *that* about?

Maybe we've had a history of too many disappointments. Or maybe we're holding onto some leftover childhood lectures and lessons: don't be selfish, who do you think you are, you're not better than the rest of us, and so on.

If we hold an internal belief that says we can't really have what we really want, then we aren't going to have it. We'll self-sabotage to make sure we don't. The judgmental bully inside of us wins every time, until we learn to face it down and quit handing over our lunch money.

That's not easy. It feels like we're in for it if we do that. Our internal judges are powerful; they invoke strong emotions – fears of punishment for breaking the rules that stop us in our tracks. Really; we're grown adults, and we feel that way.

How about we don't? We can start by being aware. If you've got that "I can't have what I want" thing going on inside of you, you might want to take 10 minutes to do a little exercise: ask yourself if you feel that way, and then write about where that belief came from. It's good to shed light on our internal ghosts – it makes them disappear.

Psychologists call that internal judgmental voice our Superego. It's the voice inside (and sometimes outside, too) that tells us to get back in line, quit whining and wait our turn (which never comes). It's good to quit whining, no doubt, but if we want to make big changes we need to break some rules, step out of line and *take* our turn instead of waiting for it.

We do that by making ourselves and what we want more important than the tattletale "I'm telling Mom, and you're going to get it!" voice that says we can't.

You might try on a new thought instead: What if what you want is a unique expression of who you are, at your deepest core? What if getting what you want is a realization of your essence as a human being? I know that sounds high-fallutin', especially if you're used to being dominated by your Superego, but just give it try.

If nothing else, it'll make you feel better, and that counts for a lot.

CHANGE WITHOUT JUDGMENT

(Part 4)
Beware: Reasons Always Win

Suppose we get past all those judgments and accusations and start moving toward the change we want. Does that mean we've put the negativity behind us for good?

No, unfortunately not. In fact, be warned: the longer we keep moving forward, the more we'll hear those judgments again and again. At first, they're bombastic and in your face. Over time, they get sneakier, camouflaging themselves as just plain reasonable and prudent common sense. Maybe you've heard some of those already: "Hasn't this gone on long enough?" "Isn't it about time you gave up this nonsense and got a real job?" "Haven't you made your spouse/ family/ friends suffer enough?"

Talk about a guilt trip.

I do an exercise in my workshops where I ask people to list all the reasons why they can't have the change they want in their lives. It's always the same list: not enough money, not enough time, I'm too old, I'm too young... and on it goes. You might take a moment and list your own reasons. Go ahead, we'll wait. Done? Okay, I can't see your list, but I *guarantee* you haven't come up with anything that someone else doesn't have on their list. I know that, because I've got a master list compiled from dozens of workshops to prove it.

If we all have the same list, then why do any of us ever even bother? What makes all these reasons so powerful that they take the wind out of our sails? Because they come with the full force of judgment. They're right, we're wrong. They're reasonable, we're crazy. And so it goes. Judgment is a powerful negative energy; it wins by making us feel bad until we plead guilty and quit trying to make the change we want.

How do we get past all these reasons and the judgment that makes them so strong? We can start by remembering three things. First, there will *always* be reasons why it's wrong for us to pursue our dreams and visions and big ideas. Always. They come with the territory. Second, they're always the same reasons, no matter what we're trying to do. And third, they're *indisputable*. They come with the full force of reason, and we can't argue with them.

In other words, these reasons are part of the landscape of change. Which means that, if they're filling your head, you're right where you're supposed to be! You wouldn't be hearing them if you weren't moving toward the change you want. You can quiet them by quitting, but you don't want to do that. So what do you do about them?

The answer will surprise you.

CHANGE WITHOUT JUDGMENT

(Part 5)
Concede the Point

State as forcefully and clearly as you can the goal you want to achieve, the idea you want to implement, the change you want to see happen. You might complete this sentence: "I want _____."

Take a moment to feel what it would be like if you made that happen. Let your imagine run with it. Stay in the feeling long enough to enjoy it.

For a lot of us, the instant we come back to "real life" after an exercise like that, we're met with an internal greeting party that tells us all the reasons why it'll never happen. The list of negatives is long and foreboding: not enough money, not enough time, c'mon this is a crazy idea, anyone can see that.... And so it goes.

What happens next, though, is *really* surprising. Most of the time, we don't just hear the list, we immediately rush to *defend* it! Instead of saying, "Hey now, wait just a minute," we *say,* "Yeah that's right! I really don't have the time/ the money/ the support. What was I thinking?"

Interesting, isn't it, the way we so ardently defend all the reasons why we can't have what we want out of life? Not only are the reasons against us irrefutable, we're on their side! We throw the book at our idea, judge it as not worth pursuing. And so we quit before we start.

Here's a simple strategy for dealing with this self-defeating urge.

First, concede the point. Agree with the accusation. "You're right, I don't have the time/ money/ support/ whatever."

Second, ask yourself, "Okay, now where does that leave me? What does life look like for me if I just drop the idea?"

Third, ask yourself: "Is this outcome acceptable? Or is there still something inside of me that still wants to give it a shot?"

Fourth, if you're not willing to give up just yet, then use your imagination to come up with a different scenario in which your idea has a chance.

We're always free to jettison the idea after step three, but if we can't do so without regret, then it's best to move on to step four and put the powerful force of imagination to work. Imagination doesn't try to win the argument, it makes all those negative reasons irrelevant. Instead of agreeing with them, we turn our efforts to creating, not debating.

CHANGE WITHOUT JUDGMENT

(Part 6)
Tension and Release

Happy New Year! Did you make any resolutions? If so, take them out and look them over. Do they contain the usual "I'm unhappy about X and need to change it or I'll be in trouble" kinds of resolutions? If so, and if you've been following this series of posts, you know I don't think they're going to work for you. Here's one last explanation why not, and then we'll move on to another topic.

We've been talking about how all those should's and ought's come loaded with judgment - against ourselves and our lives, against others, and against life itself. Those kinds of fearful and critical judgments build up a mass of unprocessed negative energy in our souls that weighs us down and impedes us from moving ahead. We need to learn to release it, and get it moving and working for us instead.

Sports psychologists talk about learning to control arousal tension and release. (No, not *that* kind of arousal and release!) An athlete or team that's too hyped up can lose focus, make dumb mistakes, and burn out too quickly. Or if they're under-aroused – e.g., if they've hit the wall or they're dragging in the fourth quarter – they need to build the energy back up.

In the same way, we can control our own internal tension and release practice in order to create sustainable change energy. If we've created negative judgment energy around our goals, we can move it out of the way by creating a sense of urgency that releases positive, change-making energy in its place. If we don't do this, those negative judgments will just pile up inside, keeping us stuck in status quo.

The simplest approach I know is to create a two-a-day habit: do two things every day to move toward your goal. You can do more if you like, but the next day you still need to do two more. Every day – write two things down, do them, cross them off (always a happy moment!), and then write two more for the next day.

That's it. Simple but powerful. Do this day after day, and negative energy has no time to build up. Instead, you're constantly moving your goal, which is its own reward.

How about you try this with your resolutions this year?

ARE LAWYERS UNHAPPY?

Part 1

I t depends who you ask.

If you ask lawyers, you'll find we're as happy with our work as anybody else: we give it about an 80% approval rating, with lawyers in government and non-profits happiest, and lawyers in private practice less so. But if you ask the media and other anecdotal sources, you'll run into a persistent urban legend that says lawyers as a whole are an unhappy lot.

A 2011 law journal article conducted a "meta-analysis" of the published research and influential media pieces on lawyer happiness over the past three decades. The results are paradoxical: on the one hand, most lawyers give their profession a thumbs up; on the other, we're more likely to engage in substance abuse and suffer from depression and other forms of mental distress than non-lawyers.

It's nice to know that we're not as bad off as the urban legend would lead us to think, at least in terms of job satisfaction, but it's disturbing to think of the economic, societal, and personal cost associated with the unhappy 20%. Plus, as the law journal article points out, it's possible for depressed and alcoholic lawyers to answer a survey saying they're happy – e.g., because of denial or lack self-awareness. If that's happening, then the 80% approval rating doesn't look as good.

Lawyers as a group are fascinating people – bright, articulate, caring, with wide interests and a drive to make an impact in one of society's essential institutions. If 1 in 5 lawyers aren't engaged in and inspired by what we do every day, then we're wasting a lot of human potential, and our clients aren't getting our best either.

There seems to be a persistent belief in our profession that lawyer malaise is just part of what we sign up for – like some kind of injury you need to walk off or put some ice on, so you can get back in the game. This engenders an sense of inevitability about job-related suffering and feelings of powerlessness about making changes. No wonder the lawyers I've known who aren't happy tend to be *really* unhappy.

I used to *live* that perspective, but not anymore. Now I believe we can rediscover our passions and make them our realities. We *can* change; it's not easy, but we can do it. And every time one of us finds the courage to do so, we take one more step toward lessening the enormous toll all that unhappiness takes on ourselves, the ones we love, and the clients we serve.

It's a New Year. If you're one of the 20%, maybe it's your year to make that change.

ARE LAWYERS UNHAPPY?

Part 2

Guess what? Happy people make happy workers! That's intuitive; there's also research to back it up. How do lawyers measure up in "happy people" derby? Not so well. Research shows that, even though we're as happy with our work as the next person, we're generally not happy people. Some people think this is because the personality traits that make good lawyers don't make happy people.

Happiness research focuses on three key factors: personality traits, personal choices, and circumstances. These weigh in at roughly 50%, 40%, and 10%, respectively, which means that 50% of us just seem blessed with sunnier outlooks on life, while another 40% can get there only by "adaptive behavior" – i.e., cultivating happiness-producing habits and an upbeat attitude.

Neither group is much affected by circumstances – including how much money they make – which factor in at only 10%. Although both groups take a nosedive from major stressors like job loss or relationship breakups, both also tend to recover to predictable "personal happiness set points," where the 50% find a customary sense of well-being which the other 40% can't reach without considerable effort.

Some researchers think the percentage of temperamentally unhappy lawyers is higher than 40%, because the very traits that incline us toward unhappiness are the same ones that account for our successes in life and our choice of law as a career. For example, the authors of the book *The Happy Lawyer* conclude that the practice of law is "disproportionately filled" with people who tend to be less happy than the general populace, citing research that shows we're more introverted and less socially connected, more doubt-ridden and inclined to consider worst case scenarios, more logical and less in touch with our feelings, as well as being achievement-oriented, aggressive, and competitive to a fault – all factors that weigh against personal happiness. If that's true, then most lawyers are part of the 40% (or more) whose happiness in the practice of law and in life can swing either way, depending on how well we adapt.

If we're not part of the naturally sunny 50%, then what can we do? We can start by realizing that, as Einstein said, "We can't solve problems by using the same kind of thinking we used when we created them." If we want to get to a newer, happier place in law and in life, we won't be able to rely on what got us here.

Giving up what's always worked for us won't be easy, even if research shows it's making us miserable. Not easy maybe, but not impossible either.

ARE LAWYERS UNHAPPY?

Part 3

Is law school to blame?

Some people think so. They propose reforms to give future lawyers a more "realistic" view of what they're in for, both in school and after. They think full disclosure will make the profession happier.

By contrast, a 2007 study found that roughly 80% of lawyers are happy with law school. That's the same percentage that says they like working in the law. So why fix law school if it ain't broke?.

How about you? What were you and your fellow students like the first day of law school, and then at the year's end? During second year? Third? From my personal experience, I'd have to say yes, something happened to us, all right. What was it?

In one study, law professor Larry Krieger and psychologist Kennon Sheldon found that entering law students are as well-adjusted as other postgraduates, but become less so as they go on. They suggest this is because we become increasingly less internally motivated and instead shift our focus to external measures of success and status – things like grades, class rank, admission to competitive clerkships, getting into law journal, etc.

In other words, we get knocked off center – we lose touch with our core values, the things we believe are most important in life. Our values motivate us, give us purpose and meaning. There's an intrinsic reward to aligning our behavior with them. Lose that alignment, and we suffer. When we lose our values, we lose our joy.

Maybe we went to law school to right wrongs, or because we were attracted to certain intellectual pursuits, or because we were after a desired economic lifestyle. So far so good, but when we shift our focus to extrinsic factors, we put our happiness at the mercy of things and people we can't control, which is why we eventually take positions we can't own, say yes to jobs we don't want, or work for clients we don't like or for causes we don't believe in. We think that makes us professionals, but unless our actions align with an internal value that supports them (e.g., we defend the unpopular client out of a sense of justice), these things take a toll.

Of course, it's possible we went to law school for all the "wrong" reasons – family expectations, misguided advice from authority figures, etc. That's another matter entirely, but regardless why we went, if we already graduated, reforming law school isn't going to help us.

What is? We can start by getting back in touch with our core values. And then we'll need to find the courage to act consistently with them. Thankfully the law is a big profession, and there's room for us in it, with our values fully intact.

ARE LAWYERS UNHAPPY?

Part 4

Formal research and media features have tried to identify just who's happy in the law and who's not. Some findings are more credible and useful than others. For example, if you graduated from the University of Virginia Law School in 1987, there's an 81% probability you were happy in the law twenty years later. Good for UV graduates, but what about the rest of us?

Lawyers in solo and small firm practice consistently rank among the happiest, as do those who work for nonprofits or in government. Lawyers over 50 are also generally sanguine, and so are most women lawyers, although the latter also leave law firms at twice the rate of their male colleagues. Racial minorities are among the happiest lawyers of all – that is, unless they're female mid-level associates in large firms.

Speaking of large firms, both formal research and anecdotal observation agree that's where lawyers are unhappiest, especially those new to the practice. One source estimated turnover among all large firm associates at 20% in any given year, and another found that 37% of new hires leave in the first three years. These percentages are even higher for associates who went to top-tier law schools – the kinds of graduates large firms like to hire.

Early career disillusionment seems unavoidable, since it can take awhile to find a practice area and setting that work for you. Maybe so, but that's still a lot of turnover. It's not surprising that one attorney and law professor declared, in a book darkly entitled *The Destruction of Young Lawyers,* that "Lawyers are pathologically unhappy."

My personal observation is that large firms don't have a corner on new lawyer disillusionment. In my firm, I told associates that their phones would start ringing with inquiries from headhunters in their third year. They were surprised when it happened. I wasn't clairvoyant, it's just that I'd gotten those calls myself.

Conventional wisdom puts the dollar cost of all that turnover at 1.5 – 2.0 times annual salary, but one commentator called this an "overly conservative" estimate "because the pool of candidates is more limited, the requirements for relative expertise is higher, and the possibility of damage to or loss of client relationships is very real."

Beyond the dollar costs, what about the costs that defy conventional metrics – e.g., the *human* cost when that many of our best and brightest are miserable? That's where the focus turns from the global to the individual. Happiness is worth celebrating wherever we find it, but that doesn't help much if you're in one of the supposedly happy categories and you're not feeling so cheery yourself.

ARE LAWYERS UNHAPPY?

Part 5: Cope or Change?

You're not happy with the course of your life in the law. Do you cope, or do you change?

There's a certain connotation to the word "coping" that gives it a sour taste, and you may have seen the recent bit on *Yahoo!* about common coping strategies that don't actually work, but coping has its uses. It can give us some short-term relief, and can set the stage for learning new thoughts, behaviors, and other life skills that help in the longer term.

Coping is less of a reach than change. We don't have to launch out on the journey of a thousand miles, we can just start taking small steps. We can learn to notice how we're reacting to things we don't like, and learn new adaptive behaviors. In the short term, a less-than-happy situation becomes more bearable, and meanwhile we're creating a platform for longer-term transformation.

After awhile, though, coping can outlive its usefulness. I came across a great quote recently (unfortunately unattributed) that helps us know when we've reached that point: "Being realistic is just socially acceptable pessimism." When coping becomes a guise for depression and defeatism in the name of being "realistic" about our lives, then it's no longer working for us. Instead, it's become a way of trying to dull the pain of a situation that will just keep eating away at our insides no matter how much we try to learn to grin and bear it.

At that point, coping turns into rationalizing, which is our way of trying to foist cheap substitute goods on ourselves. We don't accept them because we *want* to; we do it because we don't believe we can actually have what we *really* want.

So what do we do if we've reached this point? Often, we simply resign our souls over to the slow process of living lives of quiet desperation. Better if we can find a way to take the strong medicine and ask the hard questions, like the one Douglas Litowitz framed in the last chapter of his book *The Destruction of Young Lawyers*: if you're unhappy in the profession, are you going to commit to reforming it, or are you going to walk away from it?

Strong medicine indeed.

In my observation, most of us *know* when we get to that point, but the real challenge is admitting it. Plus, we don't know those kinds of things in our heads, we know them in our hearts, and we're rarely practiced in listening to the latter.

ARE LAWYERS UNHAPPY?

Part 6: **Lessons From Aristotle**

We've been talking about lawyer happiness for awhile. Aren't we getting a little carried away? I mean, yes, we live in a country founded on "the pursuit of happiness," and a lot of the guys who endorsed that idea were themselves lawyers, but that was then but this is now, so let's not get carried away.

Not so fast. How about we go back, much further back, to Aristotle – not exactly everybody's first choice as the Mr. Sunshine poster boy. Here's what Aristotle said about happiness:

Happiness is the meaning and purpose of life, the whole aim and end of human existence.

Wow. THE meaning and purpose and life, not just one option among many. Aristotle said that? Yep. Plus here's what he said about work:

Pleasure in the job puts perfection in the work.

Ever notice that people doing what they love do it really well? Think about yourself: what do you love to do – in work or in life – that you do or would do for free? How well do you do it? Really well, I'll bet.

Where *ever* did we get the idea that we can be unhappy in our work and do it well? Or be unhappy in our work and still be happy in the rest of our lives?

What if we lived in a world – and practiced a profession – where the norm was for each of us to be doing what we love to do? What would that do for lawyer happiness, both on the job and in life? Can you imagine that?

I can, and I'm on a mission to help create that world and that profession, one happy lawyer at a time. Maybe you'd like to join the cause?

What would it take? For one thing, courage. Here's what Aristotle said about that:

You will never do anything in the world without courage.

If we want that world, and that profession, we're going to have to get brave. Really brave.

Are you up for it?

MORPHIC FIELDS AND CHANGE

Part 1

We can gain useful perspective from borrowing concepts and vocabulary from other fields. Biologist Rupert Sheldrake posits the existence of "morphic fields." We can use the concept to think about how change happens (or not). Honest. Stay with me here.

A morphic field is the controlling energy field of a biological entity – either an individual or collective system. The field is made up of both organic and psychological elements. The field is invisible, but its impact is observable. For example, both genetics (organic) and individual and collective conscious and unconscious factors (psychological) invisibly affect our behavior.

Well okay then. Glad we cleared that up.

When we enter the legal profession, we enter its morphic field. Lawyers work in the *field* of law – get it? There are certain expectations, dynamics, outlooks, disciplines, judgments, commonly accepted wisdom, urban legends, etc. that come with the territory of being a lawyer. In law school, we allowed our psyches to be affected by those things – we learned to "think like a lawyer." Our neural pathways were literally rewired, our consciousness was altered, and our physiology was affected as well, so that we were biologically and chemically different beings when we graduated than we were when we started. No kidding. This brain- and body-retraining process continued when we went to work.

Within the over-arching field of law, there are also subfields that affect our experience: e.g., being part of *this* firm or *that* practice area, practicing in *this* city or *that* small town, and so on. When an individual lawyer goes to work in one of these fields, his or her individual morphic field interacts with it to create his or her experience of being a lawyer on all levels of human existence – intellectual, emotional, physical, social, and so on.

This interaction can be harmonious or dissonant. If we're dissatisfied with our work and how it's affecting our lives, it's likely because our individual field is in conflict with the field where we work. Our personal values and preferences and expectations aren't meshing with the field's: we don't like playing by its rules, don't share its values, don't like its required behaviors; don't like meeting billable hour standards or working holidays or dealing with uncivil lawyers or whatever else comes with the territory.

If we try to change our experience of work and life, then the first thing that happens is we run smack into the boundaries of our morphic fields – both our individual field, and the one where we work. Why? Because they are energetically supporting our existing reality – the one we don't want anymore, not the one we want to create.

In order to change, we need to deal with both fields. If we don't, then lack of change in one will sabotage attempted change in the other.

MORPHIC FIELDS AND CHANGE

Part 2: The game of change

Lawyer unhappiness has gotten a lot of press, and there are lots of people offering help. Usually, they emphasize either personal or institutional morphic fields, but not both. The former teach individual coping or performance enhancement skills, or offer career counseling. The latter set out to reform the legal institutions they believe are to blame.

Both strategies converge at a single choice: either the lawyer needs to change (focus on the individual's field), or the lawyer's environment needs to change (focus on the external field). This choice seems logical, but it's incomplete, and therefore change based solely on one choice vs. the other won't last. The problem is that the choice doesn't recognize that our internal and external morphic fields are interdependent, and therefore change in one means change in the other. If the changes in both fields aren't compatible, then the result is more dissonance in both of them, and the intended change will fall short.

This dynamic explains why sometimes we try to make change and end up being thwarted by self-sabotage or by external opposition, or both. It also explains why lawyers in solo practice are among the happiest, often citing as the main reason the control they hold (theoretically, at least) over their work/personal life balance.

By contrast, reformers wrestle directly with external morphic fields, such as law school, the bar exam, or the way law firms operate. Reformers derive energy from demonizing the external environment – making IT the problem. If you're a reformer at heart, this will work for you, but the key is "at heart." If that's not where your reform efforts are coming from, then the reformer approach will have the opposite effect: it will take your power away. That's because an external focus diverts your power away from what YOU need and want, and to divert power in this way is to lose it. (The great reformers also deal internally as well, but that's a topic for another time.)

Most of us aren't reformers at heart. For us, the process of creating sustainable change involves articulating our core values and desires, shaping them into goals and intentions, committing to them, and making concerted efforts to change our beliefs and behaviors to make them happen.

Doing all that is a *practice*: there are skills to learn, drills to run. But then, once we've done our reps to change our personal fields, we still need to watch how our external fields respond. The game of change is like any other game: we can practice our part only so much, but once the game starts, it takes on a life of its own, with its own dynamics. If we want to win, we do well to learn not just the fundamentals, but also how to play the game.

MORPHIC FIELDS AND CHANGE

Part 3: Abraham Maslow Rides Again

Y ou're inspired to do something BIG – so big, it's scary. And crazy as it sounds, you think you could do it, given half a chance. Now there's this raging debate inside you: are you going to go for it, or sit down until the thought goes away?

Maslow's Hierarchy of Needs can help you understand what's going on inside of you. Remember that? Of course you do, but here it is anyway:

```
                    /\
                   /  \
          Self-actualisation
        (Achieving individual potential)
               /          \
             Esteem
      (self-esteem and esteem from others)
           /                  \
          Belonging
   (Love, affection, being a part of groups)
        /                        \
        Safety
     (Shelter, removal from danger)
      /                            \
      Physiological
     (Health, food, sleep)
    /_____\
```

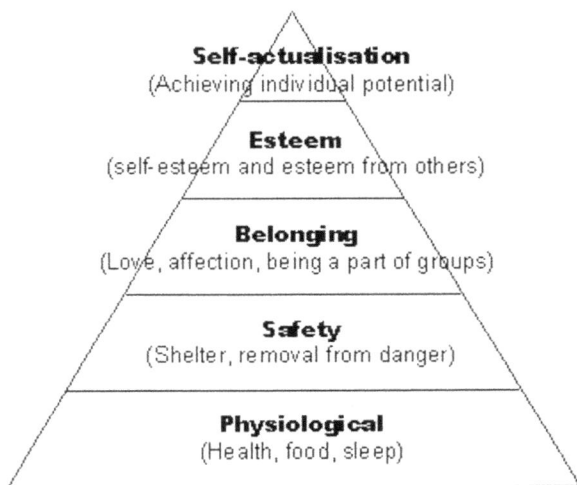

Think of the whole triangle as your psychological morphic field, and each level as a sub-field. Here's the problem: your proposed leap to the apex threatens the four bottom levels, which right now are nicely in place. You're a lawyer. Your income feeds you, puts a roof over your head, keeps the creditors at bay (especially those law school loans). You belong to a prestigious profession. You've gotten lots of strokes all your life for being a high achiever.

And now you're going to throw all that away to start a catering business or write novels? Yeah right. You'll end up alone and under a bridge. Sit down before you hurt yourself.

That's what you're up against if you want to make big changes. Right now, your psychic morphic field is in a state of what biology calls homeostasis: "the tendency toward a relatively stable equilibrium between interdependent elements, esp. as maintained by physiological processes."

Homeostasis is biology-speak for status quo; it's that state where everything is in balance. We may not always *like* how things are balanced in our lives, but *we like the balance itself.* When we think about making big changes, we threaten to throw everything out of balance, shake up the whole energy field. No wonder we freak out.

We *could* take comfort in knowing that homeostasis is a state to which nature returns, and therefore all the levels we're threatening will reorganize themselves to support our pursuit of the apex. We *could,* but we don't. We take things like our survival and safety and sense of belonging and identity very seriously. Threatening them all with one leap is just too scary.

Fortunately, there are some things we'll do even if we're afraid. That takes courage, which is not the absence of fear but action in the face of it. Courage is an essential element of any kind of change, but especially that scary leap to the top of Maslow's pyramid.

MORPHIC FIELDS AND CHANGE

Part Four: Survival of the Fittest

Ever wonder why people respond so negatively to change?

In their book *Buddha's Brain: The practical neuroscience of happiness, love & wisdom*, the co-authors – one a neurologist and the other a neuropsychologist – root our resistance to change in the evolutionary biology of the brain. Apparently our brains have been hardwired with certain survival instincts that trigger our habitual "No way!" response.

One of these instincts is the brain's version of biological homeostasis – the strong urge to keep the morphic field in balance. Our brains are constantly creating and maintaining "stabilizing systems" in their chemistry. They're like a waiter carrying a precarious stack of dishes; they're not going to like it if we mess with their balancing act. But of course that's precisely what we do when we introduce the idea of change. The result? Our brains aren't happy, and they let us know.

Another neurological survival instinct is our propensity to remember negative experiences more than positive ones. Turns out our brains learn best that way – which I guess is why we read all those cases in law school about things that went wrong. We're like the tribe who remembers the guy who ate deadly nightshade and didn't come back from the hunt. We're not doing *that* again.

These survival instincts are why the human race made it this far, and why we view new things with suspicion until we're sure they're not going to eat us for lunch.

Well okay, brains, and thanks for the help, but it's now the year 2013. There aren't any T-Rexes or saber-toothed tigers anymore, and we can find pictures of deadly nightshade on the internet. Plus, we've been at this survival of the fittest thing for a long time now. So how about we get over it and move on?

If only it were that easy. These are *survival* instincts; they come from the same fight or flight hardwiring that fires in pre-conscious nanoseconds whenever our Morphic Field Danger Alert goes off, which is surprisingly often. We think we're all grown up as a human race and past all that, but we're not – at least our brains aren't.

Fortunately, as the authors of *Buddha's Brain* also point out, we can use our *minds* to rewire our *brains*. We can cultivate new ways of thinking that create new neural pathways that embrace new perspectives about trying new things. It takes awareness and vigilance, but it can be done.

MORPHIC FIELDS AND CHANGE

Part Five: Creative Destruction

Picasso said, "Every act of creation is first of all an act of destruction." Anybody who's tried to do something new knows what he was talking about.

New exists only when old steps aside – or, to put it in "morphic field" terms, change only happens when an existing morphic field dissolves and reforms into a new one. Our bodies and brains prefer status quo, and change will eventually give them the new equilibrium they're looking for, but first there's destruction of the old equilibrium and a resulting period of chaos before a new one is reached.

Change ALWAYS begins with destruction and chaos. You'd think we'd have figured that out by now, but we haven't, so instead of welcoming Picasso's creative destruction, we react with surprise, fear, and judgment. Truth is, we're living in a shifting morphic field, where things are taking their normal and natural, biological and psychological course. That sounds reassuring, but try telling that to your rampaging emotions when you're awake at 3:00 a.m. wondering if you've screwed up your life for good this time. If the change process could be seamless, we might be okay with it. But it's not and we're not.

If we could just keep our finger off the panic button for a moment, we might remember that homeostasis is a powerful natural force that can work for us. Think of the words organic and organism; they make you think of the natural world. Now think of the words organize and organization; they connote something artificial and mechanistic, the product of human intention and engineering. Curiously, though, despite their different connotations, all four words have the same root, and represent the same natural process.

We'd like to think we can organize our organizations to work just the way we design them, but not so. For us and for them, change is always an organic process. Not only that, but we're biologically wired for constant adaptation; which means we're constantly shaping and reshaping ourselves and our environments and institutions, and so is everybody else. Which also means that, on any given day, there's a lot of creative destruction and chaos going on.

Next time we start moving toward something new and suddenly everything comes unglued, how about if instead of coming unglued ourselves, we take a moment to reassure ourselves we're just seeing the normal and natural way the old ends and the new arrives. And then take another moment to thank Picasso's ghost for the tip off.

Smart guy, that Picasso.

MORPHIC FIELDS AND CHANGE

Part Six: Balancing Analog and Digital

I recently heard a leading sports psychologist say, "Sports are analog, not digital." He was making the point that both physical and mental performance skills must be practiced, practiced, practiced, but once the sporting event starts, athletes still need to adapt moment by moment to the unplanned and unexpected. That's the way of humans, he was saying, and the way of sports.

In his book *Programmed to Run,* Thomas S. Miller, another sports psychologist and noted marathon trainer, describes our right brain as analog, and our left brain as digital.

[D]igital computers... follow exact sequences of steps, address one item at a time, and produce one solution for each problem. Similarly, the left brain deals primarily with verbal tasks, analysis, organization, planning, judgment, evaluation, and ego-speak (rational thought).

[Our right brains], on the other hand, produce an array of solutions to any one problem and are able to address several issues at one time. The right brain is best suited to run performance programs. Athletic, musical, and artistic skills, along with intuition, creativity, and imagination, are generally attributed to the right brain.

He goes on to describe how to tap both left- and right-brained functions in marathon training. We can use the same concept in the field of law, where there's a common misperception that what we do is entirely left-brained. True – the law relies heavily on left-brain functions such as language, analysis, logic, and reason, but as long as it's practiced by humans, our right brains are also still operating, serving up multiple outlooks and outcomes, and offering creative resolutions. How much we pay attention to both sides shapes the nature of our experience of the practice (whether we're happy or not) and our effectiveness.

If we want to create whole, healthy, organic, and sustainable morphic fields for our clients and ourselves, we'll embrace both sides of who we are. Trouble is, much of modern law practice management is still entrenched in late 19th and early 20th Century management theory, which was highly left-brained, mechanistic, and in sync with Teddy Roosevelt's notions of "national efficiency." As a result, law practice is often skewed to the left-brain side.

The human psyche is not so easily carved up or its functions so easily isolated without impairing the effectiveness of the whole. Lawyers are not as digital as our obsession with practice management technology would lead us to believe. We're not just hyper-connected billable hour machines. If we want whole, healthy professionals providing both logical and imaginative client solutions, we need both analog and digital. Coordinating both is the heart of sustainable performance.

RUNNING PAST OUR LIMITS 2013

Part 1: "Impossible" Takes on New Meaning

Last summer I wrote a series on lessons learned from marathon training. I'm occasionally asked for an update. Here it is, a year later.

You can read the whole story in the archives, but briefly, I started training a couple years ago as a way to deal with what I thought was an unfinished injury rehab issue. I didn't intend to become a marathoner; I was having trouble walking, running was impossible, and I'd tried pretty much everything else, so one day I got the idea of using the elliptical machines at Bally's to reprogram my body into moving again.

After a discouraging start, I eventually ran a marathon on the machine. My times quickly got faster and faster, and before long I was into elite-level training and turning in world class marathon times. No, I wasn't actually running, I was using an elliptical machine, but still… a marathon at 4:37 minutes per mile is booking it!

In the meantime, my new rehab theory wasn't proving out. The faster and further I ran, the less I could walk. It made no sense: on the machine I could do the impossible; in real life I could barely do what's possible for most people. I sought solace at the keyboard, and wrote that first *Running Past Our Limits* series, which ended this way:

> You've long since figured out that this series of blog posts isn't about running marathons on the elliptical machine. Instead, it's about running past our limits, whatever they are. It's about doing things we know are impossible. Apparently we can live in two realities at once. In one, there is no possible way we can do the thing we want. In the other reality, we can, and the first reality's negative opinion doesn't count. The first time we do it, we're stunned and astonished, and so is everyone else. The second time, it's just routine. What used to be impossible has now become the new normal.
>
> What's the new normal you'd like to create for yourself? Like I said back at the start, if all of us could tap into this idea of doing the impossible, we and our lives and our world would change, maybe overnight.

Sounds good, but the trouble was, my world definitely was not changing overnight. My first new normal goal was simply to walk again. It was joined by a second: to run a real marathon in world class speed. The second goal was happening on the elliptical machine; the first wasn't happening at all.

With encouragement from family, I began four months of bouncing from one medical specialist to another. Four MRI's, two EMG's, an endoscopy, a spinal tap, and a few dozen vials of blood later, the "impossible" I was up against suddenly took on a whole new meaning.

RUNNING PAST OUR LIMITS 2013

Part 2: Denial

When it comes to achieving goals and making changes, the inner game matters. In fact, it might be the *only* game that matters. Our thoughts and feelings create psychological and physiological states inside us that help or hinder. We can either work with that to our benefit, or not.

I got a major review course in this last February, when three huge things happened to my training: (1) I broke the "impossible" two-hour marathon mark, not once but twice; (2) during a speed workout, I "ran" a 3:34 mile that would have set a new world mile run record; and (3) I was diagnosed with MS.

Odd, isn't it, how getting tagged with a couple letters like "MS" affects us? There's an energy to them; they instantly reshape our current reality and project out a future for us. And even though February had been a record-breaking month, those two letters threatened to trash my whole training regime.

So what did I do? I went straight into denial. Let me explain. My first step was a "terms of engagement" email to friends and family. I told them the diagnosis and then laid down some ground rules: don't offer sympathy, don't tell me about people you know who have MS, don't tell me about the drugs I can take, and don't tell me to join a support group. I'm sure it seemed rude, but those kinds of responses weren't going to help me, and I needed to head them off.

That done, I dove back into training. For the first few weeks, the diagnosis often came to mind during my workouts – usually in the form of "OMG, I have MS!" The mere thought of it sucked the energy right out of me. That just wasn't going to work, so I created a patter to recite in response. Instead of "I have MS," I changed it to "A neurologist has concluded that certain conditions in my body satisfy a diagnosis of MS." My patter was factual, but the sting was gone. Whenever the MS thought came up, I'd repeat my patter to myself until the need went away. Maybe I "had" MS on some level, but I sure wasn't going to let it have me.

No, that's not Pollyannaish or positive thinking; it's actually good neurology, and was founded on medical advice. There's plenty of research to show that "fake it till you make it" has real oomph to it, plus my neurologist had said that, for a variety of reasons, drugs couldn't help, and the best treatment for me was exercise. I laughed out loud.

"I can DO that!" I said. Remember, the whole premise of my training was to fool my body into doing what it didn't think it could do. The only thing the diagnosis changed was that now I had a bigger fool to fool.

I eventually got further reinforcement for my denial approach, but not before a powerful new training assistant showed up one day.

RUNNING PAST OUR LIMITS 2013

Part 3: Opportunity Knocks

Our greatest challenges are our greatest opportunities. We don't often see them that way. Instead we get fearful and frustrated, and shut down. If we can resist that response, we'll find that obstacles are like stored up energy that, once released, launch us into our most astonishing breakthroughs. I believe and teach that, and my MS diagnosis became a case in point.

My working theory for all that gliding (fast!) on the elliptical machine was to (a) use my body to show my mind that I was capable of a running-like movement, so that (b) my mind would obligingly rewire my brain to send appropriate running signals to my body, and (c) once the circuit was complete, I'd be running again. My MS diagnosis introduced a new wrinkle: my physical training needed to do more than just change my mind and rewire my brain, it also needed it to rewire the rest of my nervous system (where the MS symptoms had taken up residence). Same plan as before, just a larger scope.

About that time, the gym where I work out installed four brand new Adaptive Motion Trainer/Open Stride machines. They're like ellipticals, with one HUGE difference: they actually require a running stride. I.e., instead of just gliding along, I actually had to pick up my feet. Since my secret for using the elliptical was that it let me get away with just gliding along, using a running motion on the AMT/Open Stride would be a giant step ahead.

I didn't see that at first; I just thought the AMT was a new kind of elliptical. I stepped on to try it out and couldn't make it move. No one else seemed to be having that problem, so I kept trying, feeling stupider by the moment, and finally asked a personal trainer for help. Just do this, she said, jogging easily along. I tried again. No luck. I closed my eyes, willing my legs to move not just back and forth, but also up and down. Slowly they started. I was exhausted after ten minutes, getting off the machine was a real problem, and walking the two blocks home even more so. All the way, I wondered, like Boromir when the Balrog shows up in the Mines of Moria, "What new devilry is this?"

Some online research revealed what an incredible gift I'd just been given. The AMT/Open Stride would teach my body perfect running form, which would get patterned directly into my brain and the rest of my nervous system, until one day I would transfer the running (not

gliding!) movement to the earth beneath my feet. Sweet!
Once again, my greatest challenge had become my greatest opportunity.

Or so I believed, but belief requires action: either the
new machine was going to get me closer to my goal or it
wasn't, and there was only one way to find out. I needed
to go back to square one, where I'd started 18 months earlier on the elliptical, with ten ponderously slow minutes.
True to form, in the months to come, those ten minutes
repeated over and over released a whole new energy into
my training.

RUNNING PAST OUR LIMITS 2013

Part 4: Find Your Placebo

My new AMT/Open Stride training got a boost when I surprised myself by going to an MS seminar and being glad I did. I'd gotten these invitations before and blew them off, but the topic was "dealing with MS through diet and exercise," and I wanted to sharpen my edge.

What I got for starters was a surprising sense of community. It was odd to watch other people do the "get up from a chair" routine, and funny to hear a speaker talk about the characteristic MS "foot slap" and "toe stub." We all laughed when another speaker acknowledged that EVERYONE views c-a-n-e as the "never-say-that-to-me-if-you-know-what's-good-for-you" four-letter word. And it was good to know I'm not the only one who's afraid I'll get stopped for public drunkenness because of the way I walk sometimes. "Just use your cane," someone said. "People will just assume you're handicapped and not bother you."

We weren't just friends in that room, we were teammates with a common goal: don't give up. One woman whose symptoms had obviously gotten the best of her – she said she was on the anti-spaz drug, and was in one of those wheelchairs that holds you upright – won a door prize and took a loonnggg time to motor herself up to the front. We didn't care, we just cheered. Plus, I saw "the look" on a couple faces. It's my game face, the one I wear when I go to my workout. It was pretty scary – both to see it and to recognize it as my own.

The highlight for me came when a medical researcher talked about the placebo effect: how people get well not from "real" treatment, but *because they believe they will.* "Find your placebo," he advised. "if you think it will help you, it probably will." I felt smug; I'd already found mine. Is it crazy to believe that elliptical marathon training will get me across a finish line? No crazier than people getting better taking placebos. I'll take another bottle of those, please, and I don't care that they're not covered by insurance.

I just finished a book called *Mind Over Medicine: Scientific Proof That You Can Heal Yourself.* The writer is Lissa Rankin, an M.D. who went kicking and screaming into non-traditional medicine after realizing that LOTS of people in placebo control groups get better. She realized that the typical attitude of "Isn't that cute, those people got better taking sugar pills" misses what she ended up viewing as the mother lode.

Plus, she goes on to say, it's not just what we believe, it's also about making room in our lives for purpose and meaning, working with passion and living with joy, getting connected and making room for creative expression, and changing our circumstances when they turn toxic on us. All these things can heal both our bodies and our lives.

And our legal careers, too, I might add.

How about it? What's *your* placebo for whatever is ailing you?

RUNNING PAST OUR LIMITS 2013

Part 5: Hold 'em or fold 'em?

Each week, my training culminates in an aggressive weekend run. My latest was epic: a marathon time just 30 seconds over the "impossible" two hour mark; 28 total miles at a 4:36 pace; plus another slow (5:18 pace) four miles tacked on at the end, just because. My body is now doing on the AMT/Open Stride machine what it was doing on the elliptical machine last February.

Compare that to the day before, when my family went to Copper Mountain to celebrate my daughter's birthday. We rode the American Eagle chairlift up, and they hiked from there to the 12,441' summit while I rode back down and shuffled around base village with my cane.

When do we stop believing, stop doing the "fake it till you make it" shuffle, stop taking the placebo, and just give up?

It's not just a question for me and my marathon training; it's a decision all of us inevitably face every time we try to create something new and big and exciting – hang our shingle, change jobs, launch a business, start an artistic project…. Hope, vision, and inspiration are strong fuel, and we run on them a long ways, but one day we hit one too many walls and run out of emotional gas, not to mention money. Now what? Do we accept our fate and go back where we came from? And what about this awful mess we've made of our lives in the meantime?

Wouldn't it be nice if we could learn when to hold 'em and when to fold 'em before things get ugly?

Jonathan Fields, a lawyer turned serial entrepreneur, author, producer, blogger, and coach, wrote a book about this: *Uncertainty: Turning Fear and Doubt into Fuel for Brilliance.* It's the best I've read on the subject, and can't recommend it highly enough. Besides his usual insights, he serves up scores of internal and external strategies for deciding when to hit the eject button or not. Three of his self-examination questions caught my eye over the weekend:

> In light of the information and experiences you've had along the journey to date, does [your] original motive still hold true?
>
> Are you still equally or even more determined to make it happen?
>
> And given what you now know, do you believe you can make it happen?

Yes, yes, and yes.

The creative journey always takes us places we didn't expect. It's by turns unnerving, threatening, unreasonable, unsafe, and just plain weird. And – what's completely exasperating about it – creativity never gets stuck or quits; it just runs on like the Energizer Bunny. Which means if anybody's going to wake up and end the dream, it's up to us.

Guess I'm not ready to do that yet. Instead, I'm looking into new ways to take my training to a whole new level. How about you?

RUNNING PAST OUR LIMITS 2013

Part 6: Mercy

I sometimes lose track of why I'm training. It's not about going farther and faster on a machine, or even about actually running a marathon. It's about reclaiming full health, in body and soul. That's the real goal; everything else is just modality.

Every creative endeavor – business, artistic, athletic, or otherwise – has times when it shifts and drifts, goes where we didn't plan, sometimes in alluring new directions. Then what? Do we reaffirm the original goal and stick with the plan, or follow the new direction to a new goal?

People sometimes suggest experimental drugs they've heard about, or theorize about mechanical gizmos that might help. Or they suggest biking or swimming instead of running. Nothing wrong with their ideas in theory (even if they would require a whole new training regime!), and if they held out a clear path to healing, I'd consider them.

But so far they haven't. Instead, they've only offered a form of dependency that full healing would make unnecessary. I don't want a drug or a device to move me; I want to do the work myself.

Maybe it looks like I'm crazy or stubborn, but something inside tells me that, if I adopted a new goal and modality, my soul would suffer. I'd give my power away; my heartfelt project would become someone else's. Never mind that their terms might produce success as they define it, I'd hurt my soul if I went there. Sorry, just can't.

It's a tough issue. Ultimately, I find guidance in the concept of mercy. I don't mean shallow "mercy rules" like everybody who shows up gets a ribbon whether they win or lose, or if the score gets too lopsided you don't have to finish the game. Those things are false mercy – bogus consolation prizes that don't satisfy. Cheap mercy leaves a bad taste – not just in our mouths but in our spirits. We lost badly and we know it. A ribbon won't change that.

Genuine mercy offers a balm to our pain. Whether we stay in the game or not, mercy invites us to create and keep creating the same way we did at first, only now our vision is clearer, we're in touch with our essence and value and purpose like we weren't before. Whether we stay the same course or try a new one isn't the point; that we can go either way with our souls intact is what matters.

Maybe mercy reveals that we didn't really want what we said we wanted after all, that we didn't fully know our hearts' desires when we started, and now the pressures and obstacles have revealed a deeper and more abiding truth about what we're after. Once we know that, there's no point staying with what would become pointless suffering. We're not quitting, we're accepting an invitation to a more deeply satisfying outcome. Quitting and mercy *feel* different, and we know the difference. Quitting mocks us because we've painted ourselves into a corner; mercy blows the roof off and shows us the stars. Quitting says it's over; mercy signals a beginning. Quitting fills us with regret; mercy stuns us with relief.

We reach the place of mercy when we pass the point of no return. Quitting can't undo what we've done, it can only make us regret we ever got this far. Mercy can't undo it either, but it doesn't want to. It doesn't call us back to what we so desperately wanted to leave behind, it invites us forward to what we really wanted in the first place. When we're in the place of mercy, it's not time to quit, it's time to begin.

That's where I'll end this update. All the denial, finding my placebo, the gift of a new training machine, the hold 'em or fold 'em crisis, and all the rest come down to just this one amazing, liberating truth: mercy, inviting me forward to new health, which is still what I'm after.

Stay tuned.

THE 2013 COLORADO
LAWYER SATISFACTION
AND SALARY SURVEY

Part 1: Look on the Bright Side

I t's no news that we flock to bad news. It's a survival mechanism: evolution has hardwired our brains to learn best by focusing on bad results – a neurological trait that seems to come easily to our profession. Accordingly, it would be easy to turn the results of a survey like this into yet another story about how bad things are for lawyers. But before we go there, let's try to look on the bright side.

For example, much of the commentary about the survey weighs the following on the positive side of the ledger:

Despite all the law school bashing that's been going on (including class action lawsuits against schools for inflating placement stats), three-fourths of respondents thought law school had prepared them at least somewhat well (49%) and in some cases very well (25%) for their careers.

Plus, now that they're part of the workforce, a full 76% said they have a career mentor to help them find their way.

Despite the talk that lawyers are chained to their desks by crippling debt, 16% reported no debt, and another 48% found their debt load to be manageable.

Despite the prevailing notion that lawyers work such long hours they can't possibly get a life, 88% said their work week comes in the "normal" range of 40-50 hours/week or less.

To get those hours, 84% worked from home, at frequencies ranging from a few times a year (31%) to once a month (19%), once a week (14%), or more (20%).

And despite how much or where they worked, 36% said their jobs rarely (31%) or never (5%) interfere with family.

Despite rumors that the Great Recession permanently turned a lot of lawyers into part-timers, a full 89% of lawyer who work in firms are full time.

84% of respondents work in firms of 10 lawyers or less, which (as other surveys have shown) are home to a disproportionately high number of lawyers who are mostly satisfied with their jobs.

And despite whatever else is going on, at least the money's good, with 83% or respondents earning $60,000 or more, 69% at $80,000 or more, and 54% over $100,000.

True, any survey at this nature invites debate about its methodology and what the responses actually tell us about lawyer satisfaction. Plus, the All-Star commentators who rolled out the survey results at the Supreme Court and wrote about them in *Colorado Law Week* have been less than fully sanguine about what the survey results tell us. Besides, who doesn't know that working at home isn't always what it's cracked up to be, or that money can't buy happiness?

We'll give those concerns equal time later. In the meantime, at least we tried.

THE 2013 COLORADO
LAWYER SATISFACTION
AND SALARY SURVEY

Part 2: "Lawyers are Stressed, Deal With It"
(The above headline appeared over one of the *Law Week Colorado* articles reporting on the 2013 Lawyer Salary & Satisfaction Survey.)

The Survey's sample size was 1,000 respondents out of a potential 35,000. Did that sample accurately represent the larger population? We can theorize about the Survey's methodology, but odds are the respondents spoke for more than just themselves. As Meg Satrom, *Law Week Colorado* editor, put it, the results "provide a good baseline on what it's like to practice law in the state."

That said, how about we shift gears and, instead of focusing on what the survey results tell us about Colorado lawyers, we ask what they tell us about Colorado clients?

If you're a client of the 1,000 respondents, and probably a larger number of Colorado lawyers, there's a good chance your lawyer:

Is suffering the effects of long-term, chronic stress. 94% of respondents said the law is stressful sometimes (48%), often (37%), or always (9%).

Didn't sleep well last night. Just shy of 2/3's sometimes (38%) or often (24%) don't get a good night's sleep, while 5% never does.

Might be sacrificing a personal commitment to make time for you. Roughly 2/3's said work sometimes (45%) or often (18%) interferes with family.

Wouldn't recommend his or her job to someone else. 61% of respondents would not recommend that somebody go to law school.

Feels financially constrained from seeking more satisfying work. 39% said law school debt has a significant effect (32%) or controls (7%) their career choices.

How's that working for you if you're that client? Or what if you live with that lawyer? Or what if he or she's a partner in your firm? Or what if you're opposing counsel, wondering whatever happened to civility?

True, not all stress is bad: in measured bursts, it energizes us to achieve, drives us to perform. It's widely accepted, however, that long-term, unabated stress is hard on us – physically, mentally, emotionally, relationally, vocationally, socially.

So what do we do about it? As noted above, one of the *Law Week Colorado* articles carried the headline, "Lawyers are Stressed, Deal With it." Okay, so we're dealing with it. We tough it out, treat it as a badge of honor that we can run full blast without all cylinders firing. Besides, we feel like we're getting by okay – a little gastro-intestinal distress notwithstanding – which probably explains why 67% of respondents don't get help with stress reduction/ management at work. Who's got time for that? It's not that we're uncaring, we're just busy people, and good for us because we're beating the odds.

Until we aren't. That's when lawyers' job stress isn't just a personal problem. When our profession stresses us to the point where a majority can't recommend our own jobs, we and the ones who depend on us are in harm's way.

And the first ones to take the hit are our clients.

THE 2013 COLORADO
LAWYER SATISFACTION
AND SALARY SURVEY

Part 3: The Ethics of Unhappiness

Okay, so lots of Lawyers are stressed and unhappy. Who cares?

If you believe what you read, apparently not lawyers. Scholarly articles about lawyer (un)happiness often begin with something like "The law is essential to society, and law is a prestigious profession." Once they've gotten *that* out of the way, they go on to lower the boom: "But our research shows that the profession shoots its wounded and eats its young." Ouch. And then they point out that lawyers themselves don't seem to mind as long as they're well paid. Ouch again.

We might wonder whether the Colorado survey results are saying the same thing. We are well paid, the respondents said, and at least we're happy about that, even though 2/3's of us wouldn't recommend out jobs to someone else.

Is trading stress and unhappiness for money just the deal you get when you're a lawyer? Maybe so: it's no secret that both leverage-based law firm economics and six-figure law school loans rely on lawyers' willingness to make that trade.

Is it worth it? Not everybody thinks so. Lawyers have opted out in various ways, and there are reform movements in law schools and bar associations trying to shake up those deal terms as well. Plus, there are relief structures in place for individuals who aren't dealing so well with their deal – such as the Colorado Lawyer Assistance Program.

All that is heartening, but self-help, reform initiatives, and relief programs all rely on a willingness to admit a problem and a commitment to change things. Trouble is – again, if you believe the research – the profession seems to have a systemic case of d-e-n-i-a-l. Plus, there are legal barriers that support a "deal with it" and "don't ask don't tell" professional culture around the topic of lawyer unhappiness. For example, a 2008 University of Louisville law review article entitled *Law Students And Lawyers With Mental Health And Substance Abuse Problems: Protecting The Public And The Individual* extensively digests all of the laws, rules, and other reasons why it can be illegal, unethical, or impolitic to ask too many questions about someone's state of mind or behavior.

Then who cares? If lawyers don't care, then maybe clients do. And if clients don't, maybe they ought to. Consider, for example, the ethics of unhappiness. The syllogism goes something like this:

Clients are entitled to competence, communication, timeliness, and sound judgment from their lawyers. If we lawyers don't deliver those things, we're unethical. Period.

Lawyers are more prone to depression, substance abuse, anxiety disorders, and suicidal thoughts than our non-lawyer clients.

Conditions like that impair competence, communication, timeliness, and sound judgment.

Take those things out of the lawyer-client relationship, and things don't bode well for either the client or the lawyer.

No, not every unhappy lawyer is an ethically impaired lawyer, but some *might* be, and any time a new survey reports high rates of lawyer job dissatisfaction, you have to wonder if it also signals the existence of levels of ethical risk as well.

Maybe the money's good, but it doesn't buy happiness... or guarantee ethical conduct.

THE 2013 COLORADO
LAWYER SATISFACTION
AND SALARY SURVEY

Part 4: Lawyers as Entrepreneurs? Easier Said Than Done

The law is a profession, but practicing it is a business. And for lawyers nowadays, the New Normal for law practice and career management is not just business, it's entrepreneurship.

So said Phil Weiser, Dean of the University of Colorado Law School, in his *Law Week Colorado* article about the Survey's results, which ran under the banner "In New Normal, Entrepreneurship a Must." In the post-Great Recession legal environment, he wrote, lawyers need to be entrepreneurial and service-oriented in a whole new way.

The other panelists at the Supreme Court roll out of the Survey agreed, but also acknowledged that, for many lawyers, getting themselves into the New Normal will be easier said than done. Radical paradigm shifts such as this one are messy, and require bold willingness to embrace change and high levels of resilience to get through it. That's characteristic of entrepreneurs, but lawyers? Not so much. "Resistance to change is endemic to lawyers," noted Patricia Powell, Dean of Students of DU Sturm College of Law. And Caren Ulrich Stacy, adjunct professor at DU Law and co-founder of *Lawyer Development Strategies*, observed that lawyers tend to be long on analytical skills and short on resilience.

That's no surprise if you consider that *lawyers get paid to be that way*, as lawyer-turned-entrepreneur Jonathan Fields pointed out in a recent blog post entitled *"Why Lawyers Make Terrible Entrepreneurs"*:

> While thousands of lawyers make the leap [into entrepreneurship] every year, it's been my observation that very few succeed.
>
> Not because they're not smart, hard-working, insanely capable problem-solvers and good people with great intentions. But because the way you are taught to think, see the world and operate as a lawyer shuts down nearly every entrepreneurial instinct.
>
> As a lawyer, a big part of your job is to forecast every conceivable thing that can go wrong for your client, then protect against it. To remove ambiguity and uncertainty. With whatever time you've got left, you focus on putting the legal structure in place to maximize the upside.

But that's nearly always second to protecting against the downside. In part, because it's often more easily quantified. In part, because that's what clients hire you to do. And, also because if you miss a major risk and things go south, you're going to share in the blame for the hit.

This "fire-walling failure" mindset is a key to your job as a lawyer. But it's total disaster for the role of entrepreneur.

These lawyer-like tendencies have thrown the door wide open for a new breed of entrepreneurial "legal service companies" like Axiom Law and Novus Law, which are growing like gangbusters as they engage in activities which most of us would agree sure look like practicing law even though the companies deny that's what they're doing. Their client service models aren't unencumbered by typical lawyer and law firm thinking. Instead, they're embracing entrepreneurship and service-orientation in ways that have clients flocking to them. Clearly, they're quite happy to be living in the New Normal.

How about the rest of us? Are we going to embrace the New Normal? And if so, how?

THE 2013 COLORADO LAWYER SATISFACTION AND SALARY SURVEY

Part 5: What the Survey *Really* Told Us:
The X Factor Revealed

Maybe the real significance of the Survey is that it brought the issue of lawyer career dissatisfaction home to us here in Colorado. Before the Survey, we were aware of other people in other places doing research and writing law journal articles and media stories about lawyer career dissatisfaction and general life unhappiness. Even the Survey's finding that two-thirds of lawyers wouldn't recommend their own jobs isn't new; it only mirrors what other surveys have already discovered. But now that we've said that about ourselves... well, that's a different story.

Not in our house, you don't!

As *Law Week Colorado* editor Meg Satrom said in her article introducing the Survey:

> Colorado attorneys should be assured that we are at least a half step ahead of attorneys in other states. While we may just be starting a conversation about job satisfaction and how we might address some of the issues facing the profession, we're well ahead of a majority of states that have yet to even begin thinking about how the profession may take shape over the coming decades.

As we've also seen, some Colorado law leaders have concluded that the Survey signals that lawyers could help themselves by becoming more entrepreneurial about their career satisfaction. Entrepreneurship is at its heart a power move. It's about stepping out of rank, insisting on new rules, seizing power. Whether you think we've got problems in our house or not, there's little doubt that those lawyers who make this power move will change the way the business of law is conducted. If you're one of those, where might you start?

With the X Factor.

I used to think you needed two things to be happy in the law:

> A fit with your practice area: finding a niche where you can attain mastery.

A fit with your practice environment: finding a place where the business of law is conducted in a way that frees you to focus on your personal vision of professionalism.

I still believe that, but now I think there's a third essential factor. In fact, I now believe this is the X Factor – the single crucial element that must be present if we hope to create sustainable satisfaction in work and in life. What is it?

Soul satisfaction: learning to work and live from your center core self – that place where your values and passions and dreams come from.

That sounds touchy-feely, but it's not. It's a discipline that can be learned and taught, that has a predictable course of development. How do we embrace it, and bring it to real-time application?

THE 2013 COLORADO LAWYER SATISFACTION AND SALARY SURVEY

Part 6: Lawyers as Entrepreneurs?
Getting Started With the X Factor.

The Survey results tell us that lawyer unhappiness isn't about working too many hours or weekends, or that we can't take personal time off or work at home when we want to, and it's *especially* not about the paycheck. Then what's making the Survey respondents so unhappy?

It's that general sense of malaise we label "stress" – that condition of our work lives that 94% of respondents said comes with the territory. Chronic and unrelenting stress is the Old Normal; it's what's been slowly sucking the life out of us. In the New Normal, stress like that isn't a given we need to put up with, it's a signal that there's something rotten in Denmark.

In her *Law Week Colorado* article on the Survey ("Could a Shift in Messaging Be the Answer?"), Sarah Clark, Counsel to Chief Justice Michael Bender, issued this challenge: "Perhaps if we focused a little less on being anxious about how much we're working, we could focus a little more on how to find meaning and gain purpose out of the nature of our work." Maybe our occupation is inherently stressful, she says, but we could help ourselves by trying to "see things a little more as they really are."

Suggesting that we'd benefit from new perspective in turn suggests that our stress might be self-generated – at least in part. How would we know? We would start by looking inside. Happiness is an inside job, and if stress is making us unhappy, it could be that our Old Normal outlook is the problem.

Gaining new perspective puts us on the path toward finding and sustaining soul satisfaction, which is the X Factor of career entrepreneurialism. Ultimately, the X Factor is less about the work we do than it is about how we're creating our work lives. That's why our quest for the X Factor begins with self-awareness.

"Self-awareness is the gentle motivator for change," a friend of mine used to say. "The unexamined life is not worth living," Socrates said. Yeah right, nice idea, but who's got time for that? Take time for "Know thyself"? Sorry, I'm pretty sure I've got something going on that night.

Who's got time for that? You do, if you want to become a New Normal lawyer. Self-awareness is your first entrepreneurial power move. Make that commitment, and your unexamined life will get examined, big time.

The quest for the X Factor isn't woo-woo, it's the hard discipline of learning to think and believe and behave differently. It's not just for the enlightened few, and it's definitely not for the disinterested or faint-hearted. And until recently, it's not something they taught us in law school. Believe it or not, that's changing nowadays, but in the meantime the lawyers who accept this challenge are mostly blazing a new trail. That can be tough, but the lawyers who master this *internal practice* are also going to be the ones who master their *law practice.* They'll be the X Factor lawyers, creating the New Normal.

That's not for everyone, but it might be for you.

CURING THE COLLYWOBBLES

Part 1: The Empire Strikes Back

"Collywobbles" is one of those delightful British words that means exactly what it sounds like it should. There are two shades to its meaning, one physiological, the other emotional:

Cramps or other intestinal disturbances.

A feeling of fear, apprehension, or nervousness.

The collywobbles are what we get when we decide to make big changes in our lives – especially if those changes affect the Big Three: career, relationships, and money. We do that, and suddenly 99.999999% of our normal competent functioning shuts down, and we retreat to what's left, which is our most basic self-preservation instinct. That instinct is unimpressed with our dreams and visions and big ideas. Its only comment is usually something like, "That's supposed to be a joke, right?"

It's no joke, and neither are the collywobbles. Gastrointestinal distress, heart palpitations, waking up at 3:00 a.m. in a panic... the mere thought of large scale change gets us into trouble. New initiatives trigger reserves of raw fear we didn't know we had in us. We should know better. Rocking the boat can't end well. It feels good and freeing and powerful for a moment, but then look out: we just woke up the Be Reasonable Gods, and The Empire of Status Quo is about to strike back.

Status quo is the combined force of everything we're used to thinking, believing, doing, and being. It's everything solid and reliable, lawful and decent and in order about our lives. Status quo makes sense of things, keeps us safe, tells us what's possible and what's not, and makes sure we don't get any ideas.

Until one day we dare to wonder, "What if...?" We're okay as long as we keep our wondering to ourselves, but as soon as we wonder out loud, we wake up the slumbering giant. Uh-oh. Collywobbles Time.

Inspiration makes us bold. Status quo makes us pay. Inspiration initiates. Status quo retaliates. Back and forth the Titans strike their blows and throw their thunderbolts. Their epic struggle is for keeps: there will be real winners and real losers, and plenty of collateral damage. The center does not hold; we go spinning off axis; our lives fly out of orbit. The seas rise and the thrones shake. We stand dumbstruck, watching the tempest from afar, when suddenly the wind shifts and we're in the middle of it, scrambling for shelter, fearing for our lives.

We've got a major case of the collywobbles.
You know I'm not exaggerating if you've ever followed your creative inspiration very far. If you haven't done so yet, but plan to, you'll soon become more familiar with the collywobbles than you ever wanted to be. You poor thing.

Why is change so hard on us? And how do we cure the collywobbles?

CURING THE COLLYWOBBLES

Part 2: Reality Distortion Field

A common source of collywobbles is the "Who are you trying to kid?!" accusation. It comes from that mean and sneaky part of human nature that's always trying to shame us back into line, and it's shockingly effective *because it just might be true:* we might really be delusional or a fraud to think we can pull off something new and different.

If we're facing that issue, we're in good company. Eric Ries, author of *The Lean Start Up,* said this in a blog post entitled *The Visionary's Lament*:

> We all know that great companies are headed by great visionaries, right? And don't some people just have a natural talent for seeing the world the way it might be, and convincing the people around them to believe in it as if it was real?

This talent is called the reality distortion field. It's an essential attribute of great startup founders. The only problem is that it's also an attribute of crazy people, sociopaths, and serial killers. The challenge, for people who want to work with and for startups, is learning to tell the difference. Are you following a visionary to a brilliant new future? Or a crazy person off a cliff?

Steve Jobs' Apple colleagues coined the term "reality distortion field" to explain his ability to convince himself and everyone else to believe whatever he wanted. A sense of reality was putty in his hands: he distorted it, shaped it to his vision of what was possible, so that people created what he wanted and bought what he was selling.

Jobs' legendary RDF was lampooned in Dilbert, and has been otherwise debunked, but it's hard to argue with his results, which ultimately is how we judge these things. As the Bud Light commercial says: "It's only weird if it doesn't work."

Accusations of insanity and arrogance come with the visionary territory. Expect them. Expect them to give you the collywobbles. But then be prepared to move on anyway. Radical departures from status quo are unreasonable and crazy, by definition. We need faith and hope – both of which have their own unreasonable and crazy downsides – to stay with them.

Former Colorado Episcopal Bishop Bill Frey once said: "Hope means hearing the music of the future; faith means dancing to it now." Yes, by all means let's dance to the music of our inspired visions, but let's also remember what Nietzsche said: "Those who were seen dancing were thought to be insane by those who could not hear the music."

How do we stay engaged when we're dancing to music others can't hear? We can start by conceding the issues raised by that mean and sneaky accusation:

Am I just making all this up? *Yes, I am.*

Am I crazy? *Yes, I am.*

Is there anything to be afraid of? *Yes, plenty.*

Am I going to do it anyway? *Yes, I am.*

Now can we get on with it?

CURING THE COLLYWOBBLES

Part 3: Of course you can't!
"What would you do if you couldn't fail?"
"What would you do if money were no object?"

People sometimes ask those questions to help you tap your dreams. They're fun to think about, but rarely effective for prompting actual change. Why not? Because there's no room in our lives for the answers. From where we sit, failure and money are *always* an issue. We know that, so after a few moments of imagining, we trade our answers for a quick trip back to business as usual.

Has anyone ever told you they'd like to hire a lawyer (maybe you) but probably couldn't afford it? I've had that issue when I've hired another lawyer to represent me, or when I've hired a consultant or coach for website development or marketing or management help or whatever. Likewise, sometimes lawyers ask me if I do individual or law firm coaching, and before I answer, they interject "but I probably couldn't afford it."

What's with that? Why the instant self-disqualification? It's for the same reason those two questions above, asked in isolation, aren't useful for creating sustainable change. The best answer to "I probably can't afford it" is "Of course you can't! Your life is organized around *not* buying that new car or wardrobe, or hiring that professional service, or whatever. You can't buy it because there's no room for it!"

In the same way, new ideas don't fit psychically, emotionally, logistically, or otherwise in your current life. If they did, they'd already be realized in your life. As it is, the mere thought of them throws a monkey wrench into your psychic machinery.

Hence a case of the Collywobbles. Hence your hasty retreat back to life as you already know it.

We're not talking here about buying new goods and services, and we're especially NOT talking about the money. This dynamic happens whenever we think about bringing new things into our lives. The price tag always includes emotional, relational, and other components. The quick dismissal is for our own-protection: we know instantly and instinctively that there's no room in *us* for all that newness.

If we want to make room for something new, the first place to create it is in our conscious awareness. To do that, we need to reckon with the lack of room in us and our lives for the new, otherwise we'll say stuck at "Of course I can't." Either that, or we'll push ahead anyway and end up with a case of buyer's remorse – the product of an over-whelmed psyche. Trying to make changes that way is like trying to stuff one more passenger into an overcrowded car. It's never convenient, there's always a lot of groaning and complaining, and everyone's happy when the ride is over.

Of course it's possible we're just hauling around too many passengers already, and somebody's got to get out to make room for the new person.

More on that another time.

CURING THE COLLYWOBBLES

Part 4: Doing the Research

We get the collywobbles from too much newness. We try to cure them by getting back on familiar, reasonable and rational ground. We do our research, hoping to convince ourselves we'll be safe out there. Trouble is, there's research, and then there's… well, the other kind.

Take observational/anecdotal research, for example. It relies on "common sense," which ought to be our first clue. Common sense says don't get carried away, make sure you have a backup plan, and all the rest. Sounds good, but it turns out what passes for common sense isn't always so sensible. You can learn why in the book *Accidental Mind,* written by a neurologist, but it doesn't take a neurologist to figure that out. We just need to remember that anecdotal research lives and dies on the assumption that all of us have our eyes wide open and can see the way the world actually works. Um, yeah, right, got it.

Then there's research that finds correlations: factors that co-vary (if one moves, so does the other), so it looks like a relationship exists. Consider for example the Super Bowl Indicator, which says the stock market will be bullish if the winner is a former NFL team, but bearish if it's a former AFL team. That metric was accurate 90% of the time for the 30 years between 1967 and 1997. Impressive, but would you bet your 401K on it? Maybe not. As one commentator said, "Anyone credulous enough to believe a football game can forecast the stock market probably should hire a money manager, or a psychiatrist, or both."

Research that shows cause and effect is the best, right? After all, science has been running on that paradigm for a long time. True, but then quantum physics came along and ruined everything by showing how observation changes outcome: i.e., we can find cause and effect just by looking for it. So much for objectivity and reliability.

Besides, cause and effect is especially elusive when what we *really* want to know is, if we do what we love, will the money *really* follow? Question: How many success stories do we need before we'll accept them as convincing data? Answer: One more than we've already got.

Then of course there's legal research: applying the law to the facts, making the best case for one side or the other. We've been doing that ever since the very first time a "think like a lawyer" neuron fired in our brains at law school, and by now we're so good at it, it's no help at all.

Besides, we're not actually doing research. What we really want is that hypothetical perfect negotiation outcome, where Life ends up with all the risk and liability, and we get a fully-secured ROI in return. Nice try. Let us know when that starts working for you.

But surely there's a way to make big change be reasonable, isn't there? I mean, isn't there?

CURING THE COLLYWOBBLES

Part 5: You can't reason your way to safety

The path of reason is not the path of change. Reason won't cure your collywobbles. It won't get you over the change threshold, and even if it does, it'll leave you hanging out to dry when you reach for it later.

Being reasonable is the way we try to understand things. If we can understand something, we can control it. Or so we think. That's especially true for lawyers: we're reasonable people, working in a reasonable profession. We are the masters of reasonableness; we are in control.

Or so we think.

Reason has its place, but not if we want to find a new career path, launch a new venture, or otherwise break out of the mold. That kind of change is inherently unreasonable. Consider the following two quotes. You know who said the first one; the second, maybe not.

Imagination is more important than knowledge. For knowledge is limited to all we now know and understand, while imagination embraces the entire world, and all there ever will be to know and understand.

The reasonable man adapts himself to the world; the unreasonable one persists in trying to adapt the world to himself. Therefore, all progress depends on the unreasonable man.

Einstein, of course, said the first one. And the second? None other than that paragon of rational curmudgeonliness himself, George Bernard Shaw. Apparently even Mr. Shaw knew his limits. Not everybody does, which is why many of the reasonable things reasonable people have said in response to proposed change are so laughable. There's a link below you can click to amuse yourself with more, but here's a quick sampling:

"Who the hell wants to hear actors talk?" -- *H. M. Warner, Warner Brothers, 1927*

"I think there is a world market for maybe five computers." -- *Thomas Watson, chairman of IBM, 1943*

"The concept is interesting and well-formed, but in order to earn better than a 'C', the idea must be feasible." -- *A Yale University management professor in response to Fred Smith's paper proposing reliable overnight delivery service. Smith went on to found Federal Express Corp.*

You get the point.

We reach for reason because we don't feel safe. Change threatens our sense of identity, our valued relationships, our income – not to mention everything else we "know" to be true and reliable. We want reason to protect us, convince us we won't end up living in a refrigerator box.

Not gonna work. We can't reason our way to safety. Reason only works in hindsight (and not always then). The Maginot Line was a perfectly reasonable defense strategy until the German Army simply did an end run on it.

Reason won't shift the playing field. It may understand and illuminate it *after the fact*, but won't shift it. What will?

For a sampling of other reasonable responses
to proposed change and innovation, follow this link:
http://www.rinkworks.com/said/predictions.shtml

CURING THE COLLYWOBBLES

Part 6: Skin in the Game

P eople in the investment banking world talk about having "skin in the game." That means, "You want our money? Then put yours in first. We're not taking a risk you won't."

Ultimately it's not about money, it's about *commitment*. Commitment requires *confidence*, which literally means "with faith." The "fidence" part comes from the same root as "fidelity," as in faith, loyalty, allegiance. Take the *fidelity* part out of con*fidence*, and all you've got left is the "con" part, as in con man. Confidence is when we speak with actions. We don't hope someone else will take the risk for us, we take it on ourselves, lay heart and soul on the line. We bet the farm. Our business clients do it all the time.

Trouble is, confidence is usually in short supply when we're in the change game. Instead of confidence, we've got the collywobbles. Weak confidence make for weak commitment, and weak commitment makes for weak results. That's not what we're after. So what do we do?

We gulp and pony up, that's what we do. It's the only surefire cure for the collywobbles. It's how we shift from a detached, dispassionate bet on an *idea* to a defining moment bet on *ourselves*. That kind of confidence doesn't hire a lawyer to make sure the other guys get stuck with all the risk. Instead, it says give me that, it's mine and I want it, because it's how I'm going to get where I want to go.

Confidence and commitment are how we get started, and how we keep going. Big projects aren't just hard to launch, they're also constantly running into insurmountable barriers, getting bogged down. They keep raising the ante, and we keep having to meet it.

"What's it gonna be?" our Big Ideas keep asking. "You in for more, or you out?" That's a rhetorical question. Backing out isn't an option. This is our shot, and we're taking it, not faking it. So we take yet another deep breath and push the chips we've been withholding out onto the table. Money, energy, commitment… it doesn't matter what it is; if we've been holding it back, we need to throw it in.

How do we find the confidence to do that? We make it up. We suspend our reason-based disbelief and go for it. It doesn't matter where we get it; what matters is that we act as if we've got it, even if we don't. We fake it till we make it. And guess what? More often than not, we do – make it, that is. It's not smoke and mirrors, it's how goals get achieved.

That's how we get skin in the game, how we act boldly, brashly even – especially when we're not feeling it.

It takes guts and it feels nuts, but that's how the change game is played.

SURVIVING A PERSONAL
APOCALYPSE

Part 1: The Four Horsemen

The world was supposed to end last year about this time. False alarm. The Mayan calendar came and went, and we never got a chance to meet (fanfare please) ...

The Four Horsemen: Conquest, War, Famine, Death. The original End Times Bad Asses – darkness, destruction, and death on steroids. If it's catastrophic, they bring it: plague, war, famine, storm, earthquake, flood, fire, raging wild animals, and a whole lot more. It's the Public Apocalypse: the worldwide bad day to end all bad days. We're all invited, and there's no "regrets" option on the RSVP card.

There's a lot of Apocalypse fascination these days – so much, that some Jungian theorists think we might have one just because so many people are envisioning it. We'll activate the apocalyptic archetype that's lodged in the collective unconscious and bring on our own end just because we're infatuated with it. Thanks a lot, Hollywood.

What gets even more play is what happens next. We know how the Apocalypse ends: the total destruction of everything. Okay, got that. But then what? What will life be like when EVERYTHING is in ruins?

Nasty, brutish, and short, apparently – judging from the books, movies, and TV shows.

But don't worry, this isn't a series about the Public Apocalypse. It's about how we live after a Private Apocalypse – after our personal lives are so completely unraveled, it feels like the Four Horsemen trampled through our living room.

The list of private catastrophes starts out like the public one – health problems, natural disasters – but also includes things like job loss, business failures, and relationship breakups. Sometimes it's a career meltdown, when we find ourselves awash in angry seas, clinging to a job life raft with a hole in it, realizing we got all the way out here for the sake of a paycheck we thought we couldn't afford to live without.

This is apocalypse on a micro level – myapocalypse. com. It's private and personal, but no less catastrophic. All is changed in the twinkling of an eye. All our boundaries and structures and beliefs have been breached. We've been shot past the point of no return, rocketed to the shocking end of the story we thought would run on forever, but we were wrong.

The post-Apocalyptic world is the land of This Was Never Supposed to Happen. There are no bearings, no context, no familiar anything, nothing but the chaos in our heads, swirling with infinite possibilities, all of them dreadful.

You know I'm not exaggerating if you've been there.

Theoretically, we could make big changes in our lives without the help of all that. We could, but we usually don't. It usually takes a crash and burn to get our attention.

It takes the Four Horsemen.

SURVIVING A PERSONAL
APOCALYPSE

Part 2: He-Who-Must-Not-Be-Named

Arch-villain Lord Voldemort of the Harry Potter stories is so unspeakably evil that just saying his name can bring his wrath upon yourself. Better be safe and refer to him as "He-Who-Must-Not-Be-Named." And keep your voice down, would you?

We have a Lord Voldemort of our own in the legal world: a possibility so scary that most lawyers won't say it to themselves, let alone anyone else. What is it? It's the idea that our next career move might be out of the law entirely.

We usually limit our options for curing the law career blues: first is to find a new job in a different practice area or environment; second is to use our legal training for something other than practicing law. There's plenty of help for either option, from headhunters and career coaches to books about what else you can do with your law degree.

Anything else is a voyage into uncharted seas, out where there be dragons. It's madness, a straight shot to Doom's doorway, a personal apocalypse waiting to happen. We have WAY too much invested the law, or at least in our legal training – financially, socially, intellectually, emotionally – to risk it. And guides are hard to find. (Although not impossible: consider people like ex-lawyers Tama Kieves and Jonathan Fields).

Sure, John Grisham, Scott Turow, and Dean Koontz all parlayed their lawyering days into mega-bestsellers, but really, how much room at the top is there? For the rest of us, to admit the possibility of getting out is to betray the profession and risk bringing its wrath upon ourselves. Lawyers just don't talk about getting out; it's an unwritten ethics rule.

Consider, for example, the torrent of angry backlash when Justice Sotomayor told Oprah that "Any lawyer who is unhappy should go back to square one and start again". (Much of the outrage derived from the crippling effect of law school loans – a sentiment that would meet with sympathy here in Colorado, where the *2013 Lawyer Satisfaction and Salary Survey* revealed that 39% of respondents said law school debt has a significant effect (32%) or controls (7%) their career choices.)

Calling our personal He-Who-Must-Not-Be-Named by its real name is not for the faint-hearted, but it might be for you. And if it is, the good news is that the stages of personal apocalypse are predicable. They've been studied and articulated. They can be taught and learned. There is a path to the Other Side of Over, no matter how Over comes upon us.

Plus, stifling our passions and dreams and visions isn't such a hot idea either. In my experience, people who might want out of the law already suspect it, but are well-practiced at holding their tongues and hearts in check. Doing that will hurt us in the long run, and might even hasten our own personal apocalypses. More on that another time.

So go ahead, say it out loud if you dare. Harry Potter did.

SURVIVING A PERSONAL APOCALYPSE

Part 3: Alchemy and a Gift for the Holidays

Renaissance physician, alchemist, scholar, and general curmudgeon Paracelsus was no picnic to be around. He was loud, opinionated, ego-inflated, and generally lived up to his middle name "Bombastus," vilifying his contemporaries' reliance on traditional texts, theories, and techniques, and advocating for fresh empirical research and perspective. But despite being personality challenged, he is credited with several lasting contributions to his field, such as founding the discipline of toxicology and introducing the notion of a mind-body link.

Robert Browning immortalized him in a poem that includes these lines:

> TRUTH is within ourselves; it takes no rise
> From outward things, whate'er you may believe.

There is an inmost centre in us all,
Where truth abides in fullness; and around,
Wall upon wall, the gross flesh hems it in,
This perfect, clear perception—which is truth.
A baffling and perverting carnal mesh
Binds it, and makes all error: and, to KNOW,
Rather consists in opening out a way
Whence the imprisoned splendour may escape,
Than in effecting entry for a light
Supposed to be without.
...
'Tis time
New hopes should animate the world, new light
Should dawn from new revealings.

What does this have to do with personal Apocalypse? A lot, actually. For starters, the word "Apocalypse" means "Revelation." (That's how the book got its name.) Apocalypse is about "new revealings" – it's what happens when you un-wrap a package to see what's inside.

How appropriate for this time of year – not just as we open holiday gifts, but as we wonder what the New Year has in store for us.

Revelation at this level isn't about your garden va-riety peccadillos. This is discovery and due diligence to the max. No secrets anymore, nothing hidden, nothing unknown. The seals are all broken, all safes are cracked, all containers ransacked and their contents strewn across a billion conference tables. All motives are revealed, all alliances betrayed, all missing links discovered. WikiLeaks is passé: all files are opened, classified access breeched, proprietary information violated. Everything has been hacked. All is Open Source.

This kind of unveiling turns us inward, invites us to realize that WE are the package opened, the mystery revealed. It's not about measuring up to external standards and practices, or the expectations and achievements of others, it's about who we are and how we're doing in our most private moments and vulnerable selves. It's about who we are and how we fit in this Brave New World where there are no secrets anymore.

Not nearly as much fun as PlayStation – more like having Paracelsus walk into the room – but in the end it's the magic alchemic ingredient that turns our leadenness into gold. Its purpose is to change both the person who lives inside our skin and the person we present to the world, make them one and the same. As such, it's the pathway to integrity, authenticity, wholeness, and freedom in the here and now.

And for that reason, Revelation is the gift I wish for you this holiday season. See you next year!

SURVIVING A PERSONAL
APOCALYPSE

Part 4: *Judgment Day*

J ungian psychology identifies observable, predictable patterns of human experience called "arche-
types." One of them is the Apocalypse archetype.
Like the others, it plays out both individually (personal
apocalypse) and collectively (public apocalypse).

Jungian scholar Edward Edinger identifies four phases
of the Apocalypse archetype: The first is revelation, which
we talked about last time. The second is judgment, today's
topic.

No, this isn't the Last Judgment we're used to hearing about, when all wrongs everywhere for all time are
thrown into the Lake of Fire, and us along with them.
Instead, as global trends analyst, futurist, and Jungian student William Van Dusen Wishard describes it, this is the
"judgment of existing beliefs and institutions against the

background of the new truth" we're given in the revelation phase.

In other words, this is the phase where we find out how our personal beliefs and behaviors, plus the operative dynamics of the important institutions in our lives, all combined to create the mess we now find ourselves in. We're going to get a private briefing on the topic, and we're not going to like what we hear. If we thought revelation was a tough pill to swallow, then our personal judgment day is like chugging cod liver oil.

As Edinger says, the judgment phase "can be so overpowering that it can threaten complete demoralization." No wonder: nobody likes to be told that the thoughts and practices they relied upon colluded with the institutions they trusted to bring about the collapse of their world. That's never happy news, and hearing it NOW makes it less so: this is after all the end of the world as we've known it, and we're not exactly having a good time here.

As a result, we usually respond by blaming others or dumping ourselves into the tank of guilt and shame and remorse. But really, there's no need for that. There's no moral judgment here, no need to punish ourselves or anyone else for what we've done or what happened to us. Forgive, yes; punish, no. It's just that there's a new sheriff in town, and things are going to be different around here. That's all. Nothing personal.

Still, the deflation is hard to overcome. We weren't trying to screw things up, weren't trying to get sick, get laid off, get hit by a train... things just turned out that way. Maybe so, but if we want to move ahead with rebuilding our post-apocalyptic lives, we need to accept responsibility for what just happened. No, we didn't and don't control everything, but we do control what we believe, how we behave, and the choices and responses we make, and now that the leases we had on all of those have been terminated – however unfairly – it's time to renegotiate. Entering those negotiations with an understanding of how we got ourselves here gives us our best shot at restoring the trust, hope, confidence, and security we've lost.

Welcome to Judgment Day. Thankfully, it's not the end of the process.

SURVIVING A PERSONAL
APOCALYPSE

Part 5: Destruction

J ungian psychologist Edward Edinger calls an apocalypse "a momentous event ... the shattering of the world as it has been, followed by its reconstitution." Hold onto that word "reconstitution" and whatever hope it gives you. You'll need it before you're done.

On the heels of that "momentous event," we're served (phase one) with the case against us: all the unpleasant revelations about how our worldview and behavior helped to bring it on. Then we hear the judgment (phase two) that not only did they bring it on, but they can't put Humpty Dumpty back together again: what we trusted in the past doesn't apply anymore; old thoughts and beliefs won't work to get us out of this mess.

Then, while we're still down and out and powerless, we enter phase three, which futurist and mega-trend spotter Van Wishard describes as "the destruction of existing beliefs and institutions that are no longer functionally an expression of the new truth" of our disrupted lives. According to Prof. Edinger, this destruction phase is experienced as "the individual's anxiety in the midst of this *transformation ordeal.*" (Emphasis added.)

No wonder we can't sleep. Ordeals aren't supposed to be fun, but this is the mother of them all.

Christopher Vogler's marvelous book on screenwriting, *The Writer's Journey: Mythic Structure for Writers,* says this about the ordeal stage of a great story:

> The simple secret of the Ordeal is this: Heroes must die so that they can be reborn. The dramatic moment that audiences enjoy more than any other is death and rebirth. In some way in every story, heroes face death or something like it: their greatest fears, the failure of an enterprise, the end of a relationship, the death of an old personality. Most of the time, they magically survive this death and are literally or symbolically reborn to reap the consequences of having cheated death. They have passed the main test of being a hero.
>
> The Ordeal in myths signifies the death of the ego. The hero is now fully part of the cosmos, dead to the old, limited vision of things and reborn into a new consciousness.

The good news is, you are the hero of your own story, and odds are excellent that you will join the ranks of countless other heroes and prevail against the seemingly insurmountable challenges your personal apocalypse has brought upon you. The bad news is, you are the hero of your own story, and you, like all those other heroes, will suffer before you reach that happy ending.

What can you do while you're in this destruction phase? Frankly, not much. Mostly, you watch, and keep breathing. Trust me – I've been there – this too shall pass. Why? Because archetypal life events like personal apocalypse really do play out to completion, and there is still one final stage to go, when the plot takes that surprise twist and the hero finally pulls it off.

We'll talk about reconstitution next time.

SURVIVING A PERSONAL
APOCALYPSE

Part 6: Float Like a Butterfly

Van Wishard describes the final stage of the apocalypse archetype as the "rebirth of belief, culture and civilized order in accord with the archetypal expression of the new truth." Edward Edinger says it's when "there begins to appear the possibility of a conscious relation to the Self and its wholeness." And here's what we get from Revelation 21: 1, 4:

> Then I saw a new heaven and a new earth, for the first heaven and the first earth had passed away ... There will be no more death or mourning or crying or pain, for the old order of things has passed away.

Got all that? Me neither. What happens after all the revelation, judgment, and destruction we've been talking

about is obviously a whole lot of New, but what precisely
does that mean, and how does it come about when the
personal apocalypse we're going through is something as
unheavenly as job loss, financial ruin, health crisis, etc.,
and there's still a lot of earthly life yet to live?

A couple suggestions. First, if we get just one thing
from the revelations of personal apocalypse, it's that we got
something we never expected, and what comes next isn't
anything we've ever known. Therefore we have no choice
but to break from the old, because the old is broken. We
need to quit, but quitting isn't easy. As Seth Godin says in
his book *The Dip: A Little Book That Teaches You When to Quit
(and When to Stick):*

> Quitting feels like a go-down moment, a moment
> where you look yourself in the eye and blink. Of course
> you are trying your best. But you just can't do it. It's
> that whole Vince Lombardi thing. If you were just a
> better person, you wouldn't quit... I'd rather you focus
> on quitting... as a go-up opportunity."

How can quitting be a "go-up" moment? Well, for one
thing, it can signal the end of apocalyptic suffering.
Consider these words, from an unlikely source:

> All experience hath shown mankind are more dis-
> posed to suffer, while evils are sufferable, than to right
> themselves by abolishing the forms to which they are
> accustomed.

"The forms to which [we] are accustomed" is what our apocalypse has gotten rid of. It's time to leave our emotional attachments to them behind. If we don't, we'll just perpetuate our suffering.

But as we go about quitting, let's not give up on myth and metaphor. They' offer powerful assistance because they grab big, universal experiences and compress them, make them intense and accessible. They work because they force us to wrestle out of them the meaning we need in the here and now.

Consider, for example, the caterpillar-to-butterfly metaphor. It's so profound and perfect that it feels like just another dose of sugary greeting card optimism, but real metamorphosis has no sweetness and light about it. The moment when the caterpillar is finally enclosed in its shroud is the moment when we can be certain there will be nothing left of it when the butterfly finally emerges, and tracing the molecular bond between what it was and what it becomes will always be cause for awe.

We don't get metamorphosis with an aggressive and willful grab, but from a willingness to believe that the bond between ourselves and our post-apocalyptic lives will be forged in the cocoon's darkness and mystery. In order to make our own personal journey to our personal "new heaven and new earth," we need to journey past our old understanding and ability and resourcefulness, to the point where all that's left is to spin the cocoon around ourselves, and make our transformation inevitable.

What could that possibly mean for you? Good question. And there's an answer already forming in the depths of your soul that's just what you need to hear. To listen will take courage, and to play it out will take vision and determination.

And speaking of which – what was the source of that earlier quote about our propensity for suffering?

The Declaration of Independence.

WINDS OF CHANGE IN
THE WORLD OF LAW

Part 1: Attorney Wellness Leaders

Google "law school wellness programs" and count the hits. Of course you'll get U of California at Berkeley (Boalt) and U of San Francisco, but hey, that's California, you'd expect that. But how about Duke, Harvard, U of Chicago... and closer to home, DU Sturm College of Law.

Lawyer assistance programs organizations like the Colorado Lawyers Assistance Program (COLAP) have changed their mission statements to adopt a far-reaching wellness orientation. They're also reaching out to law schools, with the idea of helping new lawyers integrate personal and professional well-being into their careers from the get-go.

Beginning January 1st, the Ohio Bar amended its CLE requirements to require classes in "alcoholism, substance abuse, or mental health issues, which shall include instruction on any of their causes, prevention, detection, and treatment alternatives, as applicable." Also required are classes in ethics that include consideration of "the Lawyer's Creed and A Lawyer's Aspirational Ideals."

Why am I telling you all this? Because it would be too depressing to start by telling you that CNN ran a story last month about how lawyers now rank 4th among all professions in suicide rate. The story also cited the all-too-familiar statistics about how lawyers lead the way in substance abuse, depression, and other mental disorders. Just another tiresome "lawyers are unhappy" story that won't change anything? Let's hope not – not if the law schools and LAP's and CLE Boards I've mentioned have anything to say about it.

The "Lawyer's Creed" and "Aspirational Ideals" aren't about rules and whether somebody is technically over the ethics line. They're about ideals, about how to make the world of law safer and happier, more productive and rewarding, and ultimately more competently and justly administered for lawyers, clients, judges, and everybody else involved in the legal process.

Aspirational ideals, wellness education, and assistance programs go way beyond the vague notion we picked up in our mandatory pre-graduation ethics class that somehow we're supposed to let the authorities know when somebody is struggling so much we can't ignore their behavior anymore. Instead, they're introducing a major paradigm shift so radical that it's hard to get your head around if you've bought the conventional "aspirational means optional" point of view.

Among other things, that paradigm shift is based on the stunning idea that the law can be a life-enhancing career. No, this isn't about holding hands in a circle and singing Kumbaya. It's about enlightened self-interest, about deciding that it's not okay anymore that we allow our profession to run us down, stress us out, and sometimes even kill us. It's about embracing radical notions such as the one on COLAP's webpage that says, "Problems are not a sign of failure but an opportunity for growth." That's not a surprising phrase to see on one of those motivational plaques, but as applied to high-achieving, competitive, alpha-controlling lawyers? Truly stunning.

Can you imagine personal wellness resources being part of normal life when you went to law school? I can't either. Thankfully, the winds of change are blowing.

WINDS OF CHANGE

Part 2: When Change Becomes Transformation

I t's been a windy winter in Colorado. As I write, the wind is once again blowing in another cold front. Wind signals change. Change is the Denver Bar Association's *The Docket* dedicating an issue to wellness. Change is when law schools initiate wellness programs, when Lawyer Assistance Programs adopt new, broader missions (see my last post), when bar association leaders appeal to lawyers to watch out for each other. Plus some of the other developments I'll write about in this series.

Sometimes all that's going on is a mere change in the weather, literally or metaphorically. But sometimes change is only the start, a precursor to something bigger. That something bigger is not just change, it's transformation. Transformation is when all those smaller changes suddenly stop adding up and start to multiply. Put enough small changes together, and you have a trend. Put a few trends together, and you have a movement. Let the movement gain momentum, and you have transformation.

Change is rarely welcome but usually manageable. Not so with transformation. Transformation is change that's gotten out of hand. It's the locomotive that can't be stopped, the simple act of personal conscience that erupts into social upheaval. Change presents new ideas to be tolerated and accommodated. Transformation is when you wake up one day and wonder how did it ever come to this.

Judging from the research I've been doing in connection with this series, I believe the legal profession is on the cusp of transformation. We'll see, but if so, then we're currently only in the change phase, and the big one is yet to come.

If and when it does, we're going to need a more dramatic, drastic metaphor to make sense of it. Psychologist James Hillman writes that "symbols of transformation (as birth, growth, transitions of place and time) all openly indicate a next stage. They present this next stage before the present one is over. They unfold new possibilities, affording hope."

So far so good, but watch out for what comes next. Hillman goes on to say that transformation is experienced as nothing less than death, which makes death the ultimate transformation metaphor. And the "The death experience," Hillman warns, "never feels like a transition. It is the major transition which, paradoxically, says there is no future. The end has come. It is all over, too late."

KEVIN RHODES

Consider, for example, the practices chronicled in *The Lawyer Bubble* that brought several BigLaw firms down. It's easy to read about it and feel detached and say those firms got what they deserved. But curiously, not all of them did; some continue to skate along, apparently unscathed. Such is the nature of death: the scythe swings for one but not another. And such is the nature of transformation: confusing, disorienting, unfair, inexplicable.

Transformation asks more of us than we've got to give. For some, that will be too much. We'll talk about that next time.

WINDS OF CHANGE

Part 3: When Transformation is Too Much

My wife is used to the kinds of research I do for these articles, but even she raised an eyebrow when I brought home James Hillman's book *Suicide and the Soul*. "Is there something I should know?" she asked. Yeah, I think so. I think there's something we all should know, not just about individual lawyer suicides, but also about how they mirror the collective, transformational death occurring in our profession.

Hillman called suicide "the urge for hasty transformation" – referring to the death of an individual psyche under the stress of personal transformation. In a postscript written 40 years later, Hillman added insights about the communal nature of suicide:

Once we have grasped that involvement [in relationships with others] is fundamental to the soul, we would

179

be inescapably connected by definition, turning and twisting the threads of our fate with the souls of others. Others are entangled in your death as you are in theirs. Suicide becomes a community matter.

No suicide dies or takes his life alone; the rest of the community dies and takes his life with him. We don't want to hear that. We quickly deny any personal responsibility, avoid the topic, turn away when it comes up. Hillman explains our response this way:

> This [community aspect] helps account for the common reaction against those who attempt suicide. They are not welcomed with sympathy by family, friends or clinic, but rather are met with anger and disgust. Before we sympathize with a person's plight or pain that may have occasioned the attempt, we blame; we find ourselves spontaneously annoyed, outraged, condemnatory. I do believe this all too common response points to the enduring strata of the psyche that we all share, call it our archetypal humanity. We are societal animals, as well as having individual destinies. Something insists we belong to a wider soul and not to ourselves alone.

This is why lawyer suicide stories are so disturbing to those left behind – such as the CNN story that prompted this series, or a recent story about a prominent Washington, D.C. lawyer who shot himself in his office after changing his voice mail greeting to say, "As of April 30, 2009, I can no longer be reached. If your message relates to a firm matter, please contact my secretary. If it concerns a personal matter, please contact my wife."

Can't you just see yourself doing that? I can. Change the voice mail message, set up an out-of-office email reply, write a memo about the status of pending cases… be the consummate professional to the end. A comment in that story is illustrative of Hillman's individual/community insight:

> To some his final act was a rebuke to what his beloved profession had become—a statement made in the very office he had been told to vacate.

The legal profession is a controlled access community, and once we're in the club we have a lifetime membership. ("Once a lawyer always a lawyer.") When one of our members is lost, we all lose. We can gloss over the statistics and get back to work, but we cannot remain unaffected.

Concerned bar leaders have written cautionary monographs detailing the causes and signs of individual psychological distress and exhorting us to notice who's not bearing up so well. They have their place in promoting help for the afflicted individual, but they do not reach the terminally fearful dynamics of communal transformation. For that, we need to also examine the systemic context which allowed – or maybe even promoted – that level of individual distress in the first place.

WINDS OF CHANGE

Part 4: Future Shock and the Business of Law

Alvin Toffler defined Future Shock as "too much change in too short a period of time." The book came out almost 45 years ago, the concept took awhile to gain momentum, but there's no doubt it's now in high gear. And a lot of people think the business of law is on the short list of industries likely to go the way of video cartridges and cassette tapes.

In a two part ABA "Legal Rebel" series last fall 2013, business lawyer Edwin Reeser posited that the law business is still in the throes of the Great Recession, leaving many of us not thinking clearly (i.e., in a state of *Future Shock*), and causing law firms to seek solutions in all the wrong places:

> The problem has been a lack of courage and discipline to create and deliver what clients in every industry ask

for: a better-quality product and service for a better price—to provide increased value. Firms stopped investing in people and the future of the enterprise as an institution, and they did it long before the onset of the Great Recession. We would still be facing this problem in the future, but the Great Recession accelerated and compressed it into a shorter period of time.

Not everyone is so afflicted. A stunning array of new practice models and new lawyer career paths has sprung up overnight. (A list appears at the end of an October 2013 ABA Journal article entitled *Who's Eating Law Firm's Lunch*.)

In fact, most of these newcomers aren't law firms at all, and many go way past Legal Zoom and Rocket Lawyer – two already big, big businesses providing non-traditional legal services. Instead, they live and thrive in the world of new business startups. A Valentine's Day 2014 *Tech Cocktail* post reported that funding for legal service startups rose from $66 million in 2012 to $458 million in 2013, and predicted that 2014 could be bigger. Check the math: that's nearly half a billion. And this year could be even bigger? Whoa.

Innovative as they are, those startups aren't even all the way out there on the fringe. For that, you need to check out ReInvent Law, Lex Redux, and the Forum on Legal Evolution. We're not just talking tech trade shows like LegalTech here; this the wild and wooly land of the earliest of early adopters. Their approach has two key features – technological innovation and a blunt commitment to customer service – and they go after both with a rage that isn't for the thin-skinned. As one member of the Blawgosphere said about ReInvent Law NYC:

[None of the speakers] "disagreed that the law was in crisis, change was about to destroy life as we know it, and lawyers are greedy, selfish misanthropes who brought misery to society and destruction to themselves,"

Or, as another Blawgger wrote:

[Many presenters] "dismiss[ed] the legal profession (or trade, as FMC Technologies GC [Jeffrey] Carr explained, who stated that he couldn't care less about hiring people engaged in the crime of the unlawful practice of law) as stupid and venal because lawyers have yet to recognize the one true god, technology, that will make the world a wonderful place."

Okay then.

One online comment to *Who's Eating Law Firm's Lunch* pretty well sums up the *Future Shock* impact of these developments: "Unauthorized practice of law. What Novus law is doing is illegal. None of the idiots at the ABA Journal could figure this out?"

Oh, they could figure it out, all right. But try to hold it back? Good luck with that. One commentator likened traditional law business to John Henry and his hammer picking a fight with a steam shovel. Like them or not, agree with them or not, call them illegal or unethical or not, these new bad boys are playing for keeps, and over half a billion dollars is betting on the steam shovel.

WINDS OF CHANGE

Part 5: The New Lawyer Entrepreneurs

A recent American Express survey (results announced August 2013) compared how the Great Recession affected Generation Y (age 24-35) vs. Baby Boomer (age 48-70) entrepreneurs. Guess what? It made both groups more risk averse: "just 56% say they like taking risks, down from 72% in 2007." We might have guessed.

Gen Y respondents also cited student debt load as another reason they're less inclined to risk starting a business – especially straight out of school (16% did so in 2013 vs. 28% in 2007). About the same time, a Wall Street Journal article reported that "The rising mountain of student debt, recently closing in on $1.2 trillion, is forcing some entrepreneurs to abandon startup dreams."

Average debt for undergrads is $40,000, the WSJ said, and post-grads weigh in at 55,000 - up from $40,800 10 years ago. The numbers are higher for law grads: an ABA Journal story reported that "The average 2012 law grad debt was $108,000, according to data collected by U.S. News & World Report."

Closer to home, 39% of respondents to last year's *Colorado Lawyer Satisfaction & Salary Survey* said law school debt has a significant effect (32%) or controls (7%) their career choices.

Is all that debt deterring Gen Y law firm startups? Not necessarily.

A June 2011 NBC News story profiled law grads who went solo. They did so partly in the face of a weak law job market: "since May 2008, the legal services sector has lost about 54,000 jobs, according to seasonally adjusted data from the Bureau of Labor Statistics." As a result, "the number of recent law graduates going solo increased from 3.5 percent in 2008 to 5.5 percent in 2009, the biggest one year jump since 1982" (citing data from the National Association for Law Placement).

It's not just the bad job market that's fueling the startups. The AmEx story reports that Gen Y entrepreneurs take the leap primarily to pursue something they feel passionate about. Armed with that passion, they launch themselves with a characteristic can-do attitude, pushing growth though social media, rewards for repeat customers, and effective use of technology.

The new lawyer entrepreneurs are cut from the same cloth. As one of the lawyers in the NBC News story said:

> I don't need a big copier, I don't need a huge support staff to manage all my paperwork and I don't need an expensive phone system. Basically I just need a laptop and cell phone and I'm off and running.

Another caters to entrepreneurs like herself, using a virtual office and a secure client log-in system. She says this:

> There have been times when I've woken up in the morning and I have new clients. They've found me online somehow and I've never had any interaction with them, but now they're my clients. It's pretty sweet.

And speaking of can-do attitude, one law school graduate paid off his $108,000 in law school debt in four years. His strategy? "All I had to do was put my life on the line," he said. Not exactly what you'd normally think of as entrepreneurial, but equally innovative and focused.

Did they learn any of that in law school? Some did, some didn't. We'll talk about that next time.

WINDS OF CHANGE

Part 6: Learning to Think Like ~~a Lawyer~~ an Entrepreneur

A June 2011 NBC News story profiled law grads who went solo. They've got hutzpah, no doubt:

"I say screw the economy. You worked hard, you got your law degree, so make something happen with it."

Where did they learn the entrepreneurial ropes? Not at law school. Here's what they said about that:

Law schools are not equipped to help you start your own firm.

I love some of the classes I took at [law school], but virtually none of them are useful.

Considering this amount of debt and that most classes deal with theory rather than everyday, practical law... three years of law school are unnecessary and should be shortened.

There's a whole economic engine behind law practice and to not get that business side of it in law school sucks.

That's not the case everywhere. The NBC News article tells this story:

When Dr. Silvia Hodges first proposed a "Law firm as a business" course, Sheila Foster, the associate dean for academic affairs of Fordham University School of Law, was skeptical.

"I wasn't completely convinced that was a subject that our students would catch on to, so I asked her to further develop the concept," Foster said.

But Hodges remained persistent. Now students consider the law firm management class and the law firm marketing class Hodges recently began teaching among the most useful courses at the school.

"Just having that technical knowledge is not enough in today's world anymore. They need a more well-rounded picture," Hodges said.

Chetson agrees, saying that if law schools really want to place their students in good jobs, they need to teach them to be self-sufficient.

Closer to home, I was recently interviewed by a CU Law student as part of an assignment for a class led by Dean

Weiser, in furtherance of his commitment to promoting the "New Normal of legal entrepreneurship.

Private initiatives have also stepped up to fill the gap. Solo Practice University bills itself as "The *Practice of Law* School" that "picks up where your law education left off." It offers web-based instruction and opportunities for virtual networking. The Lawyerist blog is chock full of practice management how-to's. There are others, too – a whole new industry forming around the need to educate and support legal professionals as the practice of law reinvents itself.

The days of hiring law students who've been taught to think like lawyers and hoping they'll learn business development and practice management skills by osmosis are over. The winds of change are blowing; they're bringing in a sea change. Some lawyers are embracing it, and some are literally dying from it. How about you? Are you sails up, or are you battening down the hatches?

(For those who might be interested, a couple new ABA publications related to topics I've been writing about in this series came to my attention this week. One is about reinventing the practice of law, and the other is about different generations working effectively together.)

THE PRACTICE OF LIFE

Part 1: The Ethics of Happiness

I've written before about the ethics of unhappiness, describing how stressed-out lawyers pose ethical risks, especially when their unhappiness reaches the point of depression and other stress-related disorders. Today, let's look at the positive side – brought to us, appropriately, by the discipline of Positive Psychology.

As a teaching fellow, Shawn Achor helped to create the famed Harvard "happiness course." Now he's a globe-trotting consultant, taking Positive Psychology principles to companies worldwide. In his book *The Happiness Advantage*, he makes the case for happiness in the marketplace, starting with an upside-down look at the topic:

> If you observe people around you, you'll find most individuals follow a formula that has been subtly or not so subtly taught to them by their schools, their

company, their parents, or society. That is: If you work hard, you will become successful, and once you become successful, then you'll be happy. This pattern of belief explains what most often motivates us in life.

The only problem is that this formula is broken.

[N]ew research in psychology and neuroscience shows that it works the other way around. We become more successful when we are happier.

When we are happy – when our mindset and mood are positive – we are smarter, more motivated, and thus more successful.

It turns out that our brains are literally hardwired to perform at their best not when they are negative or even neutral, but when they are positive.

(Emphasis in original)

This isn't Pollyannaish theory; it's backed up with psychological research, neuroscience, and real-world business experience:

Data abounds showing that happy workers have higher levels of productivity, produce higher sales, perform better in leadership positions, and receive higher performance ratings and higher pay. They also enjoy more job security and are less likely to take sick days, to quit, or to become burned out. Happy CEOs are more likely to lead teams of employees who are both happy and healthy, and who find their work climate conducive to high performance. The list of benefits of happiness in the workplace goes on and on.

What this means for the legal profession is that happy lawyers are more likely to deliver the best of the competence, communication, timeliness, and sound judgment we're ethically obligated to provide. It also means that the best-performing law firms – the firms that will also make the "best places to work" lists – could be founded on a single guiding principle: promote lawyer happiness.

Think about it.

For most of us, happiness is a learned skill. Again, as Achor says:

> The Happiness Advantage... is about learning how to cultivate the mindset and behaviors that have been empirically proven to fuel greater success and fulfillment. It is a work ethic.

I.e., it's a *practice*. We can practice happiness like we practice law, except that if we put lawyer happiness at the core, we'll create a practice of law unlike anything seen before.

THE PRACTICE OF LIFE

Part 2: Getting Started on Getting Happy

This series is about happiness as a success strategy. Before we go on with it, here's a quick update on a post a couple weeks back about lawyers learning to be entrepreneurs.

Last week I attended a CLE on *"How to Manage a Small Law Firm."* It's on a sponsored national tour, and offers training in the business of law that's more systematized and supportive that you get with DIY. The following blurb from the CLE brochure shows its connection to our current topic of happiness:

Law firms that are well-managed make lawyers happier. Law firms that are well-managed help lawyers act in a manner more becoming a professional. Law firms that are well-managed also tend to be more profitable than those that are managed by the seat of one's pants, especially if those pants have never sat through even a single course about how to manage a small law firm.

The company behind this offers training, events, connections, workbooks, practical help. You might check them out. And now, moving along....

The Great Recession (Really? What was so great about it?) has been officially over for years. The Miami Herald and other media outlets have produced scores of articles on the Great Recession's indelible impact on the business of law.

Many lawyers and law students are still feeling the aftershocks. One of those is the psychological condition of "learned helplessness." Here's how positive psychologist Shawn Achor describes it in *The Happiness Advantage*:

> What I've learned from many companies I've spoken with over the past two years [writing in 2012] is that the meltdown of 2008 and its aftershocks had instilled a form of learned helplessness – a belief in the futility of our action –in many of the world's workers.

Learned helplessness is when we know there are things we could do to help ourselves, but we simply can't summon the energy or resolve to execute on them. Then, once a hopeless and helpless outlook takes root in one area of our lives, it seeps over into all others. Again, from *The Happiness Advantage*:

> And it doesn't end [with work]. When people feel helpless in one area, they not only give up in that one area;

they often "overlearn" the lesson and apply it to other situations.

How do we reverse this insidious way of thinking? Positive thinking isn't enough. Summoning lost willpower doesn't work either. We can post inspirational quotes on the refrigerator door all we like, but we can't rally around them. For example this one from Jim Collins' *Good to Great*:

> We are not imprisoned by our circumstances, our setbacks, our history, our mistakes, or even staggering defeats along the way. We are freed by our choices.

Inspiring? Yes. True? No doubt. But helpful? Not necessarily. It's like our self-help circuit got disconnected, and all the motivational sayings in the world can't reconnect it. Now what? We're sick of the pity party, we're not about to blame a recession, we want to get moving, but how to start?

The way back begins with self-awareness – admitting that that this is a real issue for us. Yes, eventually we'll need to find the resolve within ourselves to go on, but sometimes it's just good to know we're not alone. No need to beat ourselves up. It's not just a personal problem: this odd inability to help ourselves is a malaise of our times – millions of workers *around the world* are feeling it. Just knowing that gets us out of ourselves, which means we can start to deal with the issue objectively.

The Happiness Advantage gives us some specific strategies for dealing with our learned helplessness. We'll talk about them next time.

THE PRACTICE OF LIFE

Part 3: Taking Back Control

One thing lawyers are up against in the Happiness Derby is that things can look good on the outside. Being a lawyer is prestigious, and looking good doing it maintains not just our professional status but the neurological state of homeostasis (status quo) our brains love so much.

We'll give up a lot to maintain professional status – even our happiness. Trouble is, when we sacrifice our happiness we lose our edge, which leads to diminished performance, which impedes success. Too much of that, and one day we find ourselves in the state of "learned helplessness" we talked about last time.

Once we're there, it's easy to start pointing fingers – at colleagues, staff, clients, law firms, law schools, the judicial system. We get a perverse short-term benefit from blame-shifting – we don't have to take the hit for what's bugging us – but it isn't worth the long-term cost to our happiness. Blaming others gives them power over our work performance and our personal wellbeing: *they* have to change before *we* can be happy, and *we* could be waiting a long time.

Instead of thinking, "The practice of law is making me unhappy," how about if instead we think, "I am an unhappy person." Maybe unpleasant to admit, but at least now we've got our control back. We can't control the externals, but we can do something about the person looking back at us from the mirror. (Anybody else's brain just cue up Michael Jackson's "Man in the Mirror"? Just asking….)

In his book *The Happiness Advantage,* Positive Psychologist Shawn Achor describes the importance of this shift from external to internal focus:

> [T]he most successful people, in work and in life, are those who have what psychologists call an "internal locus of control," the belief that their actions have a direct effect on their outcomes. People with an external locus, on the other hand, are more likely to see daily events as dictated by external forces.
>
> One of the biggest drivers of success is the belief that our behavior matters, that we have control over our future.
>
> Feeling that we are in control, that we are masters of our own fate at work and at home, is one of the strongest drivers of both well-being and performance.
>
> Interestingly, psychologists have found that … gains in productivity, happiness, and health have less

to do with how much control we actually have and more with how much control we think we have.

After all, if we believe nothing we do matters, we fall prey to the insidious grip of learned helplessness...

Too many unhappy lawyers get all the way to learned helplessness by keeping up appearances. The way back starts with admitting that appearances won't help us get our mojo back. For that, we need to start with the man (woman) in the mirror.

We'll talk about practical steps for regaining control next time.

THE PRACTICE OF LIFE

Part 4: Getting Your Mojo Back

C areer mojo gone? Life mojo missing? Want it back? Getting your mojo back starts with self-awareness: admitting you're not lighting it up the way you'd like. It's tempting to shrug off this step, short-change it. Don't. This series has been quoting from *The Happiness Advantage;* let's go to the well once again:

> Experiments show that when people are primed to feel high levels of distress, the quickest to recover are those who can identify how they are feeling and put those feelings into words. Brain scans show verbal information almost immediately diminishes the power of those negative emotions, improving well-being and enhancing decision-making skills.

Think about it. Feel it. Write about it. Keeping a journal is not self-indulgent, it's an effective way to discharge negativity, which by definition has an immediate, positive impact.

Next, find something you can control, and tackle it by *thinking small*:

> Once you've mastered the self-awareness [step], your next goal should be to identify which aspects of the situation you have control over and which you don't.
>
> One of the biggest drivers of success is the belief that our behavior matters, that we have control over our future. Yet when our stresses and workloads seem to mount faster than our ability to keep up, feelings of control are often the first things to go, especially when we try to tackle too much at once. If, however, we first concentrate our efforts on small manageable goals, we regain the feeling of control so crucial to performance.

We waste energy on big picture drama when we're in the doldrums, and end up feeling overwhelmed and indecisive. Thinking small refocuses our energy:

> The point is to tease apart the stresses that we have to let go because they're out of our hands, while at the same time identifying the areas where our efforts will have a real impact, so that we can then focus our energy accordingly.
>
> Once my trainees are armed with a list of what is indeed still within their control, I have them identify

one small goal they know they can quickly accomplish. By narrowing their scope of action, and focusing their energy and efforts, the likelihood of success increases.

Lost mojo means lost confidence. Thinking small builds it up again:

> Setting smaller, more manageable goals helps us build our confidence and celebrate our forward progress, and keeps us committed to the task at hand.
>
> By first limiting the scope of our efforts, then watching those efforts have the intended effect, we accumulate the resources, knowledge, and confidence to expand the circle, gradually conquering a larger and larger area.

Thinking small also builds momentum:

> By tackling one small challenge at a time – a narrow circle that slowly expands outward – we can relearn that our actions do have a direct effect on our outcomes, that we are largely the masters of our own fates. With an increasingly internal locus of control and a greater confidence in our abilities, we can then expand our efforts outward.

Think small – it's simple, accessible, high-leverage. Quick success creates fresh confidence. Before you know it, you're ready to tackle the bigger issues. We'll look at a couple of those starting next time.

THE PRACTICE OF LIFE

Part 5: Managing the Mask

Wearing a professional mask is one of the tools of our trade. We don't do that out of hypocrisy, but to meet the demands of our work. We've got a lot to do. Our masks keep us on track. We need that.

Here's what psychologist Edward Edinger says about the benefits of professional personas, both to ourselves and the society we serve:

> Now of what value is awareness of the persona to the individual and society? Here again, as with all self-knowledge, both the individual and society benefit. You see, it commonly happens that, to a greater or lesser extent, one is identified with one's persona. It is so convenient. It is hard enough to acquire competence in a professional career, and once that has been

achieved, the satisfactions of that achievement are so significant that there is a strong tendency to identify with that professional role.

The minister learns an appropriate persona as he goes through theological seminary, and then starts his first job as assistant pastor; the medical student learns the medical persona; the lawyer learns hers, and so on. And once that is learned, things work so smoothly when operating out of it that there's a strong tendency to identify with it. But the trouble is, for society as a whole, that when one meets one's doctor, or one's pastor, or one's lawyer, or whatever, one isn't meeting a full human being. You meet the mask.

All that is understandable.... [I]t takes too much time to be real. It is much easier to function out of your [professional] persona. The great advantage of it, though temporary, is that it doesn't take any effort, you don't have to respond out of the deeper human realities. So you can get more work done in a day.... It takes much more time to listen... and respond humanly, and then you get way behind in your schedule.

From Edinger's book Science of the Soul

So far so good, but it's not hard to spot the downside. there is more to us than our professional masks. There are times when we need to take them off, when we need to "be real" and not be identified with our professional persona, when other people need to meet "a full human being" and we need to respond to them "out of the deeper human realities" of who we are.

Managing the mask begins with self-awareness. As Prof. Edinger says "If self-knowledge is to proceed and if individuals are going to achieve a full, well-rounded personality, it is important that they realize the reality of the persona." Wear the mask or don't wear the mask, but do so consciously, because "it makes a world of difference whether you're doing something consciously or unconsciously, because choice is involved."

There's that word "choice" again. Choice is essential to regaining that sense of control we've been talking about – which in turn is essential to promoting our happiness, both on the job and away from it.

THE PRACTICE OF LIFE

Part 6: Facing Down the Saber-Toothed Tiger

The *2013 Colorado Lawyer Satisfaction and Salary Survey* showed that most Colorado lawyers (a) work under the kind of chronic stress that hurts us in the long-term, but (b) put up with it because they're well paid. Lots of other scholarly research and media articles have said the same thing.

In other words, one of the things that can stand between lawyers and happiness is the money they make. 83% of Survey respondents reported earning $60,000 or more, 69% were at $80,000 or more, and 54% were over $100,000. Those are strong numbers. So what's to complain about?

If you're not happy, the numbers don't help. Turns out that "money doesn't buy happiness" is more than a folksy saying; it has roots in neuroscience. Our *minds* know that being happy and making money aren't mutually exclusive.

Our *brains*, on the other hand, aren't so sure. They'd rather play it safe and take money over happiness any day.

Why do our brains do that? Once again quoting positive psychologist Shawn Achor and his book *The Happiness Advantage*:

> Neuroscientists have found that financial losses are actually processed in the same areas of the brain that respond to mortal danger. In other words, we react to withering profits and a sinking retirement account the same way our ancestors did to a saber-toothed tiger.

Did he just say that our brains react to financial stress the same way they would if we found ourselves face-to-face with a saber-toothed tiger? Yes, that's what he said. It's a neurological fact that money issues light up the most basic survival-instinct parts of our brains. Mess with our paychecks and our fight-or-flight mechanism kicks in. Adrenaline pumps through the system; we get busy surviving.

No wonder, then, that the Great Recession hit the business of law so hard. It hit us where it hurts: in our above-average pocketbooks. That was bad enough on financial terms, but the source of our distress and disorientation goes much deeper. Making good money helps things look good on the outside, and therefore maintains a happiness-depleting external locus of control, at the expense of a happiness-enhancing internal locus.

That shift in locus is why, in our minds a least, a well-paying job trumps happiness. Pit happiness against money, and we're not talking prestige anymore, we're talking survival. And *that* is why we eventually take on the mindset of learned helplessness that kills happiness. This doesn't happen because our priorities are screwed up; it happens because our brains are wired that way.

Fortunately, we can use our *minds* to alter our *brains'* automatic "put up and shut up" response. Which is why knowing the tiger is still on the prowl has motivated many lawyers to seek new, sustainable solutions to the business of law. (In case you missed it, we looked at several of them in the last series.)

Going inside ourselves to cultivate happiness becomes a practice of *life* that's good for our souls, good for business, good for professionalism. And none of that requires taking a smaller paycheck. In fact, as we've also seen, cultivating happiness might just create a larger one.

ENLIGHTENMENT MADE SIMPLE

Part One: Simple, Not Easy

N irvana, bliss, paradise, enlightenment... what would that be for you? Yes, you. And not on some ethereal plane, but in the life you actually have, right here, right now. Better yet, what would it be like if your career and life *as a lawyer* were enlightened?

I watched a group of 30 North Dakota lawyers answer that question for themselves earlier this week. (Well, not *exactly* that question, but a series of questions that got to the same point.) They wanted less stress, more peace, more freedom and autonomy, more meaning, satisfaction, fulfillment, purpose. If that's not enlightenment, it'll do until the real thing comes along.

I did the same workshop for a group of non-lawyers last Saturday, and the responses were the same. They're always the same, no matter the audience. We all want these things, but few of us feel we have them or believe we ever could.

Does that mean enlightenment is unattainable? I don't think so. These are universal desires; why would we all keep wanting what we can't have? Surely evolution would have knocked this foolishness out of us long ago.

Assuming it's possible, how do we get there? It's simple, really: learn to live on the other side of ego. Here's the Einstein version:

> The true value of a human being can be found in the degree to which he has attained liberation from the self.

Or if you prefer a more enigmatic quote from a more spiritual source:

> Enlightenment is ego's ultimate disappointment. -- *Chögyam Trungpa, Tibetan Buddhist, Founder of Naropa University*

By ego, I mean the dynamic organizing principle that gives our lives psychic shape and physical expression. Psychologists tell us ego is fully formed by age 4; after that, it acts like a gravitational center, drawing our experiences into orbit around itself, defining for us what's normal and what's not, what's safe and possible and predictable and what isn't. Ego gives us our sense of self, creates boundaries that differentiate us from others, lays down our foundational beliefs and habitual behaviors. It creates and sustains who we are, what we do, and what we have. Ego accounts for how we make decisions, our likes and dislikes, our areas of competence and ignorance. And a whole lot more.

We need all that to survive in a scary world. Until we don't anymore, and we realize that, for all its usefulness, ego hasn't given us what we really want – freedom, fulfillment, and all the rest. That's when it's time to learn to remove ego as the gravitational center of our lives.

Simple? Yes. Easy? No. But not because it's complicated. It's only hard because we've never been there before, and don't know how to get there from here.

We can learn. Honest. But before we start, it's good to heed some practical advice:

> The road to enlightenment is long and difficult, and you should try not to forget snacks and magazines. -- *Anne Lamott, from her book* Traveling Mercies: Some Thoughts on Faith

ENLIGHTENMENT MADE SIMPLE

Part Two: Evolution's Case for Enlightenment

We wouldn't want enlightenment if we couldn't have it. All those things we called "enlightenment" last time – less stress, more peace, more freedom and autonomy, more meaning, satisfaction, fulfillment, purpose – are there for the taking.

At least, evolutionary neurology thinks so. I found that out recently when I tackled a stack of books on the subject. The books weren't exactly a beach read; they went back to the library mostly unread, but not before leaving me with two astounding bits of awareness.

First, creation evolves. That's a fact – not a desire or aspiration, not a random shot in the dark, not a maybe or a guess, but a fact. Every created thing is encoded with an irrepressible urge for growth, change, improvement, progress.

Second, evolution is efficient. It doesn't waste itself on what isn't going to happen. It plays its hand carefully, places bets where the odds are good. No, it's not infallible, but its batting average is enviable.

Put those two ideas together, and that's why enlightenment is possible for all of us, not just for people who can sit in the lotus position. "Life, liberty, and the pursuit of happiness" aren't just political ideals, they're an evolutionary impulse evident in the wide world and embedded in the human soul. That dynamic isn't only in us, but in everything we create – personally, professionally, artistically, and otherwise. We were born this way, and we endow everything we create with the same energy.

Which is why we're going to see more *Star Wars* movies.

You've heard the quote, "'Whatever the mind can conceive and believe, it can achieve." Napoleon Hill said that in his 1937 self-help classic *Think and Grow Rich*. I confess – that's another book that went back to the library mostly unread. Maybe the book isn't my cup of tea, but the quote is neurologically defensible: if our brains have evolved to the place where they can hold big ideas about how wonderful our lives can be, then they're probably ready to take on the project.

We quickly dismiss our big ideas as pipedreams. We might want to rethink our practice, suspend our skepticism, and entertain those ideas instead. The notion that they might become reality isn't just positive thinking, it's a possibility supported by evolutionary neurology. Maybe we can't get all the way to the top of the mountain just by thinking positively, but we can make a start, knowing the odds of getting there are probably better than we think.

If enlightenment is so possible, then why don't we just grab it? Ah, not so fast, Grasshopper! Probably we don't leap into the arms of bliss because we know it's going to cost us. We talked a little about that last time. We'll talk more about it next.

ENLIGHTENMENT MADE SIMPLE

Part Three: Why ego has to go

Ego is why we believe what we believe and act the way we act. Ego is in charge of deciding what's normal and possible, and one thing it knows for sure is that the kind of enlightenment we're talking about in this series is neither.

Ego sounds authoritative, but feels a lot less so when you realize that, on a cellular level, it's the aggregate of our brains' most commonly used neural pathways. As we saw last time, if our brains can conceive of the idea of a life and a career filled with happiness and fulfillment, they're ready to give it to us. Neuroplasticity - the brain's ability to rewire itself - can actually trump ego, and make impossible things happen.

That's a hopeful thought, but it doesn't make it easy to let go of ego. Ego got the corner office because of its track record. It kept us safe when we were kids, navigated us through adolescence, made sure we got things done when we grew up. No problem with any of that, but that's actually the point.

Ego is our life regulator. As long as it stays in charge, it's business as usual. If we're not experiencing life the way we want, that's because our ego structures aren't buying into the idea. And guess what: *they never will.* Ego is a one-trick pony; it won't and can't learn; all it can do is execute its ideal of how things are and ought to be. If we want something new, we need new neural pathways to replace the ones currently in charge. The corner office needs a new tenant.

I've used this quote from Einstein before, but it's so good, why not do it again:

We can't solve problems by using the same kind of thinking we used when we created them."

He might have substituted "the same ego" for "the same kind of thinking." Ego is embedded in our life experiences (including the one we're having right at this moment, reading this). Want more of the same? :Let ego keep its job. Want change - not little change, but **BIG** change? Then it's time for the severance package.

We'd like ego to keep its job because we're used to it and think it can change. Not gonna happen: the list of ego features that need to change is just too overwhelming.

Our Intellect – particularly the different kinds of intelligence we do or don't use;

Our approach to relationships at work and home;
The beliefs we hold about how life works, what's important and what's not, etc.;
Our sense of identity and meaning and purpose;
Our learning style;
Our decision-making style;
Our likes and dislikes, areas of knowledge and ignorance, competence and incompetence.
Etc. etc. etc.

When our quest for enlightenment runs into resistance, we blame ourselves, blame life, blame Fate, blame the gods.... Better to simply acknowledge that the brain wiring that supports ego is just humming along the way it always has. We can stay stuck in ego, or we can go ahead without it, but one thing we can't do is teach it new tricks.

We'll talk more about that next time.

ENLIGHTENMENT MADE SIMPLE

Part Four: Accept No Substitutes

"Something else is possible" is the simple, powerful, and essential belief that gets us into the enlightenment game. With it, we can move toward peace, freedom, autonomy, meaning, satisfaction, fulfillment, purpose... whatever makes up our version of enlightenment. Without it, we won't get started, and won't continue if we do.

Holding that belief isn't easy, because ego doesn't believe it, and as long as it's in charge, we're not going anywhere. That's why ego has to go, like we saw last time. That's simply said, but not easy to do.

Our brains support our egos by creating and maintaining a "road most traveled" of neural pathways for our habitual thoughts and actions to run on. It's a very neat and tidy and efficient system, until one day we come stomping in with our muddy boots on its newly-waxed floor and announce we just saw the light.

What happens next isn't going to go well.

Ego trots out The List of All the Irrefutable Reasons why we can't, don't, and won't get what we want. I've been asking for that list in workshops for the past four years, and it's always the same. You can recite it with me: not enough money, it's a bad time, I'm too young, I'm too old, my firm/boss/spouse isn't going to like it, etc., etc.

The. Same. List. Always. Everywhere. Every crowd. Every time. It's ego-generated, and it's a stopper. No matter how pumped we are about making change, once ego weighs in, the game is over.

Each of us thinks our list is personal. It's not. The reasons are universal. Think about it, if it's always the same list, then how could change ever be possible for anyone? It's an obvious question, but we don't ask it. We give up instead.

It's not that we're wimps, it's just that reasons always win, and no wonder: they're backed by fear. Fear of what others will think. Fear of failure. Fear period. We sense that, and we back off, rationalizing why it's a good thing if they win the argument, forgetting that it's ultimately *an argument against ourselves.*

Rationalizing is ego foisting cheap substitute goods on us. We accept them not because we want to, but because we believe we can't have the real thing. Rationalizing tries to make a bad thing sound good. Consolation prizes are the most misnamed trophies in the world. They mean well, but they don't help. There's no consolation in them; not to our hearts, anyway. Maybe they placate ego, but we still feel lousy. We were in it to win, but we lost, and we're hurting. Where's the consolation in that?

No dream of what our lives could be at their highest and best should have to suffer that kind of indignity.

Ego is not an original thinker. Substitutes are all it has to offer. If you want enlightenment, then get it. Period. Adopt and enforce an Accept No Substitutes policy. Hold out for the good turtle soup, and forget the mock.

Just know that working with the recipe is going to require some tinkering.

ENLIGHTENMENT MADE SIMPLE

Part Five: Pivoting on the Path to Paradise

W hen we start down the Path to Paradise, we lay our "Life Capital" on the line: we stake what we've been and done and have on a dream, a vision of what could be. It's a bold, risky, scary venture. We'll run into big time challenges, and to meet them we'll need to stay light on our feet, be adaptable, flexible, resourceful. And we'll need to do that without compromising, rationalizing, or otherwise losing the essence of what we're after.

How do we do all that? By learning to pivot.

Pivoting is a term borrowed from the entrepreneurial world, where the idea is to create continuous feedback loops that monitor market response to innovation. You want to know what works in real time, and you want to find out before you blow through your startup capital.

Eric Ries, author of *The Lean Startup*, describes pivoting this way in his blog, *Startup Lessons Learned*:

In a lean startup, instead of being organized around traditional functional departments, we use a cross-functional problem team and solution team. Each has its own iterative process: customer development and agile development respectively. And the two teams are joined together into a company-wide feedback loop that allows the whole company to be built to learn. This combination allows startups to increase their odds of success by having more major iterations before they run out of resources. It increases the runway without additional cash.

Increasing iterations is a good thing - unless we're going in a circle. The hardest part of entrepreneurship is to develop the judgment to know when it's time to change direction and when it's time to stay the course. That's why so many lean startup practices are focused on learning to tell the difference between progress and wasted effort. One such practice is to pivot from one vision to the next.

So how do you know it's time to change direction? And how do you pick a new direction? These are challenging questions, among the hardest that an early startup team will have to grapple with. Some startups fail because the founders can't have this conversation - they either blow up when they try, or they fail to change because they are afraid of conflict. Both are lethal outcomes.

I want to introduce the concept of the pivot, the idea that successful startups change directions but stay grounded in what they've learned. They keep one foot in the past and place one foot in a new possible future. Over time, this pivoting may lead them far afield from their original vision, but if you look carefully, you'll be able to detect common threads that link each iteration.

Pivoting is disorienting because when you do it, it's hard to tell if you're still moving toward your vision or if you're giving up on it. The key to "learning to tell the difference between progress and wasted effort" is to stay in touch with those "common threads that link each iteration." In enlightenment terms, that means staying anchored in the purest distillation of what you're really after, and allowing the rest to fall out as it will.

ENLIGHTENMENT MADE SIMPLE

Part Six: Micro-About Pivoting

(For more about entrepreneurial pivoting, check out The Art of the Pivot *in the May/June 2014 issue of Inc. Magazine.)*

We rarely seek enlightenment and the things we want from it — peace, meaning, fulfillment, and all the rest — for their own sake. We're not in the habit of doing nice things like that for ourselves. Instead, we justify our quest by embracing some noble and idealistic and altruistic vision. We'll make life better for ourselves, but we'll also help someone else while we're at it. Thinking that way gets us off the dime, makes us willing to defy the odds and the gods.

It's a good way to start, but it won't sustain us, especially when the resistance we meet makes it obvious why we haven't done this before, or why we failed when we tried. Not that there's anything wrong with wanting to make an impact in the world, but those ambitions take their cues from outside ourselves: we're focused on changing some-*thing*, instead of changing some*one*, namely the person who lives inside our own skin. As long as we maintain that external orientation, our status-quo-loving and change-resistant brains will be quick to turn tail when things turn tough.

And they *will* turn tough. Enlightenment is an inside job that's harshly unsympathetic to whether the externals are lining up to support our grand visions. In fact, it's usually the case that we've barely taken a few baby steps when the path to Paradise plunges us into the cavernous muck where ruined dreams rot.

We need to pivot in order to move on from that place. In physical terms, pivoting is rotating around a still central axis. In entrepreneurial terms, pivoting is what we do when we find out the market doesn't want our brilliant ideas. In enlightenment terms, pivoting is what we do when we find ourselves wallowing in the mess we created in the name of doing something awesome with our lives. Entrepreneurial and enlightened pivoting rotate around the center of what we're really after and who we really are. The externals spin and blur, but not the core.

Our enlightenment quest takes us to that core. Along the way, we detach from ego, which is necessary because, if truth be told, our plans to save the world were probably just a spiffed-up version of ego. Ego is immobilized down in that creepy chasm; it becomes dead weight we need to jettison if we're going to make it through. And often, when we get rid of ego, the vision goes with it.

That doesn't mean our grand visions won't ever come to fruition. They might, but you can bet it won't be the way we originally envisioned, or because ego wrangled them into being. If they come to pass at all, it will be because they resonate deeply with our core selves. Find that core, and pivoting is both possible and powerful: execute that one swift, nifty move, and suddenly we're unstuck and unleashing whole new worlds of creativity that make surprising things happen.

Then another wonderful thing happens: enlightenment hands us our bag of swag, full of peace, freedom, and all the rest. And we find ourselves living the truth of that inspirational saying that it's not about making change happen, it's about becoming the change we wish to make.

(And by the way, was that a paraphrase just now of something Gandhi said? Or was it Thoreau? Or maybe Nelson Mandela? If you're wondering, you'll enjoy this article about what they *really* said, and where those inspirational sayings *really* come from.)

ENLIGHTENMENT MADE SIMPLE

Part Seven: Micro-Brewed Bliss

The last two posts in this series were about pivoting. A few decades ago we would have talked about guerilla marketing. More recently, the topic would have been the nimble organization. Nowadays, you probably know about the microenterprise movement, you've noticed all the Colorado microbreweries and wineries, and you've probably seen stuff online about microhousing. Long before any of that, we had *Small is Beautiful*. Plus variations on the theme along the way.

That adds up to four decades of thought leaders telling us the same thing: our world isn't supporting monolithic monuments to status quo anymore. There's just too much change going on. Centralized, formalized, institutionalized "corporate cultures" can't stay relevant and responsive. Globalization has paradoxically both homogenized world culture and shattered the "market" into a gazillion shards, where it's indie-this and indie-that, micro products delivered to micro markets.

What does all this have to do with our desire to live fulfilled and meaningful and satisfying lives? Lots, actually.

For starters, it's evidence of a systemic pivot that's running through human existence -- an evolutionary neurological adaptation playing out on billions of micro-stages. Consider this quote from a blog post entitled "Nimble: The New Big."

We define organizational nimbleness as the ability and willingness to make smart and timely decisions about core organizational strategies, resources and actions based on real-world dynamics.

Consider what mind scientist John Medina says about human history and our ability to adapt: "How, then, did [humans] go from such a wobbly, fragile minority population to a staggering tide of humanity 7 billion strong and growing? There is only one way. You give up on stability. You don't try to beat back the changes. You begin not to care about consistency within a given habitat, because such consistency isn't an option. You adapt to variation itself."

Less stress and more peace, freedom, autonomy, meaning, satisfaction, fulfillment, purpose, and whatever other qualities of experience we put in our enlightenment bags aren't about settling down, getting low and slow. Not so in a world where a single new product announcement can wipe out a whole industry, and dealing with "Big-Bang Disruption" is part of a CEO's job description.

If we want personal and career enlightenment in the year 2014, we need to "adapt to variation itself," which means staying light on our feet, nimble, ready to pivot. We need to go micro, create meaning in small, powerful doses, while simultaneously sticking to "core organizational [and personal] strategies." In other words, we need to embrace chaos while staying centered.

That's a lot to ask the human race. We were just getting comfortable in our evolutionary recliners. ("Hey, grab me some more self-actualization while you're up, would you?") And it's especially a lot to ask the sector of the human race that makes its living in the legal profession, where precedent is our shared genome. No, we're not all hidebound -- as we've seen in past blogs about "disruptive innovation" in our profession -- but most of us aren't exactly early adopters either.

Is the prospect of enlightenment worth all this chaos and disruption? How do you find peace in the midst of chaos? Even Bob Dylan had his reservations: ""I accept chaos," he said, "But I'm not sure whether it accepts me." Are those dreams of enlightenment more trouble than they're worth? How bad would it be to just hunker down into ego and enjoy a decent paycheck and let the Avant Garde do the crashing and burning for the rest of us?

Good questions. We'll tackle them next time.

ENLIGHTENMENT MADE SIMPLE

Part Eight: Is it worth it?

We want purpose, meaning, autonomy, happiness, and all the rest of what career and personal enlightenment have to offer. We also want getting them to be safe, easy, and certain. We don't want to rock the boat. We want to be able to look around and know where we are. We want to be able to do the things we've always done, think the way we've always thought, but just be happier about it.

In other words, we want enlightenment to *be* different, but we also want it to *feel* as safe as the life we're trying to leave behind.

Where in the world did we ever get such an idea? From ego. From the survival instincts lodged in the most ancient part of our brains. From our brains' embedded practice of maintaining status quo. And from the collective expressions of those things in the organizations, cultures, firms, and other institutions that make up the milieu of our lives.

Challenge all that in the name of greater satisfaction and happiness? Better think twice. It's not going to go well. Status quo gets old, but so does constantly having to create our chaotic new lives in the name of making them better. It's fun at first, but eventually it feels like all we accomplished was to trade one kind of stress for another. It's possible to get past that point, but a lot of people never do, it's just so entirely demoralizing.

For some crazy reason, life is set up so the pursuit of enlightenment is optional. We can get it, but it'll cost us, and the cost is high: we have to end the reign of ego. Most people won't do it. Most people probably shouldn't. Better for them if they don't turn pro in the enlightenment game. Better if they keep the day job, don't cash in the 401k.

That's not cowardice. Nobody says you have to do this. After all, ego and status quo are effective: they get the job done, pay the bills. We challenge them at our own risk, and the people who do aren't exactly good role models.

Ever notice that so many of the people we admire live unbalanced lives? It costs a lot to do be who they are and do what they do. They're the creative fringe, the radical, aberrant few. They left the safe center of the bell curve behind long ago, and now they're statistically irrelevant, three or more standard deviations out. They're out there on the edge, delusional by any standard of normalcy. They're no longer productive citizens -- at least not as status quo measures it. They take irrationality to new extremes, become a danger to themselves and others. They think "getting a life" is overrated. They work too hard and don't know when to quit. They're often not likeable or fun or safe to be around.

They're also the creative leaders we've always needed in our world, and need again right now.

And who knows, you might be one of them.

RUNNING PAST OUR LIMITS 2014

Part One: Time to Get Personal (Again)

The past two years, I've taken a summer break from topics like lawyer career satisfaction and legal entrepreneurship, and instead have gotten personal. The first year, I worried about doing that, but justified my departure from objectivity by telling myself I'd stumbled onto something so powerful it could change the world. Honest. I was using it to meet a challenge in my own life, but thought it was much bigger. (Actually, I still do.) The series told my story, but also talked about believing in ourselves, finding our internal "coach," doing the impossible, and other inspiring things. A couple readers said they thought it was my best series ever.

Changing the world wasn't the focus last year, mostly because I'd learned that the challenge I face goes by the big hairy scary name "MS." I focused not on changing the whole world, just my world with MS. Still, getting personal was okay because there were plenty of lessons to extrapo-late to other kinds of challenges, and again readers liked it.

At a recent CLE seminar, I got one of those intuitive hits to share some of my Running Past Our Limits story. My departure from the script paid off: it was an energiz-ing moment (right after lunch!) that drew several com-ments on the eval's.

Do something once, it's a novelty; do it twice, it's a tradition. So here's the Third Annual Running Past Our Limits Update.

Briefly, this adventure started because I was frustrated with what I thought was an unresolved injury rehab issue. I'd tried pretty much everything to no avail, until one day I got the idea of using an elliptical machine to reprogram my body into moving again. (Where do we get crazy ideas like that, by the way? We'll talk about it.) In the first year, I ran several marathons on the machine, some at world record speed. By the second year, however, it was clear my rehab theory wasn't proving out: the faster and further I ran, the less I could walk. I went to get checked out, and found out I have MS. Immediately I went into denial, deter-mined to fight the disease (if I even had it, which I wasn't willing to admit), and doubled down on my workouts.

And this past, third year? (Take a deep breath.) Even though I'm not in denial anymore I'm still not ready to give up, although to be honest it gets harder all the time, but there's some cutting edge neurological research to back up what I'm doing, and in the meantime my workouts and what I've learned from them have turned into a whole new way of approaching life that has made it better in ways I never could have imagined, not to mention giving me all kinds of new insights I regularly use in this blog and in my workshops... and did I mention that some people have gotten inspired by what I'm doing?

Against that background, the real question for me at this point is:

And I'm supposed to be okay with that?

Seriously, am I just making lemonade because life gave me lemons, reaching for the consolation-less consolation prize I warned you not to accept in a post not long ago? And what's the difference between conceding defeat/failure and the practice of pivoting I've been talking about? And how DO you move from denial to acceptance without giving up?

Good questions. Let's tackle 'em.

RUNNING PAST OUR LIMITS 2014

Part Two: A day (and week) in the life of an MS Athlete

Someone told me about MS Fitness Challenge. Great organization; you should check them out. The founder David Lyons is in showbiz, so they get a lot of celebrity endorsements. David did a terrific interview of me for his blog. I just looked at it again, and it gave me the idea for this post.

All MS athletes share symptoms that would stop us if we let them. The trick is to make them irrelevant. Well-meaning people at the gym sometimes ask how I'm feeling, whether I'm having a good or bad day. I've learned to pause and explain that I don't think in those terms. They aren't helpful. If I paid attention to how I feel, I'd never show up, and I sure wouldn't keep going when it gets tough.

And it does get tough. You do this, you suffer. Not whining, just sayin'.

The MS symptoms create practical challenges beyond the workout itself, too -- like getting off the machine when I'm done. I can barely walk; it takes all my focus to cross about 20 feet to sit down. I drag myself along and hope nobody is noticing, and one time I took a facer. Lately I've been wondering if I should just bring my cane. Same thing with walking down the stairs to leave the building. These days I mostly take the elevator.

I work out 5 days a week on average, with goals for every workout and for the week. I alternate strength, stamina, and speed workouts, and something I call "heart elasticity" training. (Did one of those yesterday. Two hours all out. Looked like I was standing under a rain spout, which is something for a guy with MS, because one of things you lose is your body's ability to cool itself. Guess my training has reversed that.)

The differences in workouts are a matter of metrics: varying machine settings such as stride height, length, and resistance, and watching how they interact with body metrics such as stride frequency, target heartbeat, breathing pattern, even how much I sweat. On stamina runs I can zone out, but the other workouts require constant attention, changing the machine settings and monitoring body metrics.

Daily workouts are a couple hours, weekends take longer, but training is really 24/7. It's a whole, integrated practice embracing details like how much I sleep and when and what I eat. Mostly, there's an action/recovery cycle to be observed. Cut corners, you suffer. Like I said....

The weekly cycle culminates in a major weekend work-out. This past Sunday I went three hours, in one-hour segments. The first was for speed, the second (my fastest, as is usually the case) for combined speed and strength, and the third for stamina. Around 2:50:00 I hit the point where my right foot spazzes out so entirely it turns out like a ballet dancer's. I've learned to pull it back straight by sheer focus, and can keep it there for 20 minutes; on Sunday I only had to deal with it for the final 10.

The Open Stride machine is stingy about mileage: best I can tell, it credits just under half what a regular elliptical machine gives you. Sunday it gave me 15.35 begrudging miles -- not much to show for 3 hours and 2,000 calories. Curiously, when I go that hard that long, my feet and legs often work better than they do after a shorter workout. That was the case yesterday.

So I took the stairs instead of the elevator.

RUNNING PAST OUR LIMITS 2014

Part Three: Mission Impossible

A friend who'd been involved with making a documentary film got interested in my running regime. We shot a video one fine day last October. It's short: 7:15. Go ahead, we'll wait while you watch it (http://kevin-rhodes.com/whats-your-impossible-video/).

The video begins with me challenging our conventional notions of what's possible and what's not. "Impossible is just a label we put on things," I say. "It's state of mind. There are people doing impossible things everyday. I think it's time we all stop believing in impossible."

The idea that "impossible" might not be hack-proof was first embedded in me at a Cirque du Soleil show called *Varekai,* which premiered a year and a half after 9-11. The *Varekai* story is loosely based on the *Icarus* myth: the manmade wings and failed flight too close to the sun, the familiar parable of the human race outstripping its own aspirations and crashing down in its pride.

Yes, humans can't fly like birds; we all know that. But *Varekai* went beyond the myth and ended in triumph. Pride was forgiven, love and courage restored the fallen, and the joy of aspiration and the magic of the dream were reclaimed. The impossible became possible.

Dominic Champagne, writer and director of *Varekai*, began his program notes with these words:

> Puisque les temps sont fous/ *Since these are crazy times*
> Et que nous avons le devoir/ *And it is our duty*
> De ne pas abandonner le monde/ *To not surrender the world*
> Aux main des nullités/ *Into the hands of fools*
> Je fais le vœu que ce spectacle soit pour vous/ *I wish that this show may be for you*
> Comme il a été pour moi/ *As it has been for me*
> Une celebration/ *A celebration*
> De la rencontre des fraternités/ *Of the coming together of friends*
> Et de la joie des dépassements/ *And of the joy of challenging limits*
> Pour dire au monde/ *In order to tell the world*
> Que quelque chose d'autre est possible/ *That something else is possible*

I put those program notes in a frame that still hangs on my wall. I live them everyday. They inspire me, keep me centered, keep reminding me that *something else is possible.*

We want things that appear to be impossible. Maybe they aren't. Maybe the only reason they're impossible is because we haven't done them yet. Okay, so we ran a search of our brain's memory data base and it came up "no match found." No big deal. That doesn't mean what we want is impossible on some grand cosmic level; maybe it's a possibility waiting for us to make it happen.

I feel that way about my personal impossible of overcoming MS with exercise. I'm sure the other people in the video felt that way about their impossibles, too. And yet they did them, just like I intend to do mine.

The video ends with a series of questions: How about you? What's your impossible? What would you be like if you did it? What would our world be like?

If you haven't done it yet, go ahead and watch the video now. You'll be inspired, I promise.

RUNNING PAST OUR LIMITS 2014

Part Four: Running Just Because

And sometimes you run just because.

Forget the inspiration, the challenges, the training techniques, the goals.

Forget researching neurology for scientific support. Forget constantly recalculating the odds, feeling like they get worse every day, wondering how much life this experiment has left in it.

Forget all that. This morning, just be that 12-year old racing a friend home after a Friday night small town football game, suddenly noticing that his feet aren't even touching the ground and he's leaving the fastest kid in town far behind.

Or just be that 17-year old running wind sprints on the football field and coming in just a few yards behind the fastest kid ever to play running back in your town, the holder of three conference championship records as a sophomore, and all the coaches are looking at their stop-watches and saying, "Who's that kid in second place?"

Or just be the kid the varsity track coach pulls aside one day and says, "You're built just like Jim Ryan -- we should make a miler out of you."

That conversation never went any further. Every now and then I wonder what might have happened if it had, and I always end up being glad it didn't, because like Jim Ryan I might have walked off the track in the middle of a race one day.

But never mind any of that, not now. Just be who you are, right here, right now: a kid's soul living in an adult's body. Step on the machine and you're out of that body, running like your younger self, running for the pure joy of it. All the struggle and trying to figure things out fade and fall far behind, like the fastest kid in town who couldn't keep up with you. There's nothing but the movement, nothing but the stride, over and over, churning up the invisible ground under your feet. Machine metrics? Who cares? Moving is all that matters.

Your heart swells, you're just so grateful you can do this.

Jim Ryan had the perfect stride. I've studied it frame by frame. I visualize it when I run on the machine, pat-terning my brain, telling it, "Make me look like *that*."

This past Sunday, I looked like *that* for two hours and ten minutes. It was only during those last ten minutes that I noticed the machine was telling me my heartbeat was up in the "high performance" category, that my right foot was starting to spaz out and turn sideways, that I was feeling tired.

It didn't matter. I was running. My long legs were put on this planet to run; there's no other explanation for them.

And so, this past Sunday, that's what I did.

I ran.

Just because.

RUNNING PAST OUR
LIMITS UPDATE

Part Five: A Random Idea Gets Scientific

In the video I told you about a couple posts ago, a friend of mine (his name is "Angel Vigil" -- no kidding) describes my workout routine as "his own self-invented alternative treatment to keep the nerves and his muscles and everything working as long as he can, and fight the progressive, debilitating nature of MS."

Angel didn't know it, but he was summarizing two neurological concepts that underlie what I'm doing. The first is neuroplasticity: our brains rewire themselves when we learn. The second is myelination: if we use those new neural pathways often, our brains coat them with a substance called myelin, which acts as a learning and skill development supercharger.

Developmental molecular biologist John Medina describes neuroplasticity this way in his book *Brain Rules*:

Eric Kandel is the scientist mostly responsible for figuring out the cellular basis of [the process of how the brain learns]. For it, he shared the Nobel Prize in 2000… Kandel showed that when people learn something, the wiring in their brain changes. He demonstrated that acquiring even simple pieces of information involves the physical alteration of the structure of the neurons participating in the process. Taken broadly, these physical changes result in the functional organization and reorganization of the brain. This is astonishing. The brain is constantly learning things, so the brain is constantly rewiring itself.

Myelination got a huge popular boost from Daniel Coyle's 2009 book *The Talent Code.* As the Amazon book blurb says:

Drawing on cutting-edge neurology and firsthand research gathered on journeys to nine of the world's talent hotbeds—from the baseball fields of the Caribbean to a classical-music academy in upstate New York—Coyle identifies the three key elements that will allow you to develop your gifts and optimize your performance in sports, art, music, math, or just about anything.

These three elements work together within your brain to form myelin, a microscopic neural substance that adds vast amounts of speed and accuracy to your movements and thoughts. Scientists have discovered that myelin might just be the holy grail: the foundation of all forms of greatness, from Michelangelo's to Michael Jordan's. The good news about myelin is that it isn't fixed at birth; to the contrary, it grows, and like anything that grows, it can be cultivated and nourished.

Put neuroplasticity and myelination together, and you've got brain flubber. Both are at work in our brains all the time, whether we know it or not. My approach is to harness them consciously and intentionally. Technically, what I'm after is re-myelination -- when damaged neural pathways get rebuilt. I need that because MS has a destructive effect on -- you guessed it -- myelin. Therefore, in neuroscience terms, my exercise routine is an attempt to use neuroplasticity and re-myelination to restore my MS-damaged neuro-pathways.

Just like Angel said.

I didn't know any of this three years ago when I began my "self-invented alternative treatment." I just had an idea. Turns out I got the idea about the time neuroscientists were hot on the myelin trail. Apparently I somehow got on somebody's memo routing list.

Now that I *do* know about these things, I have a new goal in life: to become a lab rat.

More on that next time.

RUNNING PAST OUR LIMITS 2014

Part Six: Science and Snake Oil

A friend shared a TED talk with me about how a rat with a severed spinal cord had its nervous system regenerated so it could run again. The researchers used a combination of chemical and electrical stimulation to get the rat's legs moving involuntarily, but that wasn't enough. So they created a robotic harness that allowed the rat to move if and when and where it wanted. After that, the rat's spinal cord grew new connections. The scientists created an opportunity for healing, but the rat's desire to move took over and made it a reality.

No wonder some scientists built a statue to honor a lab rat. God bless that rat. It's my hero; I want to be just like it. We all know you can't move again after your spinal cord is severed. The rat proved us wrong. We also know you can't win a marathon if your MS makes it hard to walk. How about if I be the lab rat who proves us wrong?

The rat needed scientific help, and so do I. Seriously, now: if by any stretch you know someone who is seriously researching MS and exercise, would you please email me with an introduction? Let me be honest: I don't want ideas, like have I contacted the National MS Society. If you can think of it, I probably have already. What I'm looking for is a real relationship handoff to a real person. If you can do that, then many, many thanks.

Once we've got a research lab on board, we need a committed rat. No problem there. The rat introduces the X Factor: how does the desire to move generate healing? The scientists don't know, and the rat's not talking. If it could, it would probably sell us snake oil, and we'd probably buy.

Last year I wrote about the "placebo effect": believing yourself into an altered state in which the healing you want actually happens, even though it's not supposed to, there's no rational reason why it should, and you're actually putting your faith in a sugar pill.

I know one guy who got rid of his MS by visualizing miniature beavers chewing up his brain scarring ("Multiple Sclerosis" means "multiple scarring"). I'm not making that up. If that's not a placebo I don't know what is. I've haven't tried his approach, but I'm not above a daily practice that includes mind tricks, even though I honestly believe some of what I do is pure snake oil.

Is it still a placebo if you don't think it will work? The authors of a book on personal growth called *The Tools* answer that question by telling this "famous story about Niels

Bohr, the great Danish physicist and father of quantum physics":

> A young physicist visited him in his home and saw a horseshoe hanging on the wall over the hearth. "Surely, professor, you don't believe that a horseshoe will bring you good luck," the young physicist exclaimed. "Of course not!" Bohr replied. "But I've heard that you don't have to believe in it for it to work."

(If you're like me and wonder if this story is apocryphal, check out http://quoteinvestigator.com/2013/10/09/horseshoe-luck/. Sounds valid to me, both because Niels Bohr was quite a quotable guy, and because the story is in the spirit of quantum physics. Moving right along....)

And so we've got science, and we've got snake oil. Should work.

The next installment will be the last in this series. We'll tackle the feeling that time seems to be running out on this experiment, and then we'll be done.

For this year, at least.

RUNNING PAST OUR LIMITS UPDATE

Part Seven: Life in an Alternate Reality

There's a scene at the start of my running video where my wife and I are walking along, with a voiceover saying I never really wanted to run a marathon, I just wanted to be able to go on walks with her like we used to.

I can't do that anymore. Walk like that, I mean. We shot that scene about ten months ago, and I can't do that anymore.

When I saw my neurologist six months ago, I told him I've been surprised at how quickly my physical abilities are degenerating. It's like there's a timer running. I'm awesome on the machine at the gym, but when I walk it feels like time is running out. And running? Time ran out on that a long time ago.

That's my reality. Or is it? No it's not, but you already knew that. I don't like living with that timer, so I relegate it to an alternate reality. Einstein said, if the facts don't fit your theory, change the facts. That's what I do.

The alternate reality with the timer is persistent, though. It wants to know how long I'm going to keep fighting, why I don't just give it up as a lost cause. The people at MS Fitness Challenge have the fighting spirit. They inspire me, but I'm aware that fighting causes stress, and if what's going on in your body is degeneration, you don't need more stress. So instead of fighting, I relegate the timer to its alternate universe, and go on living in the reality I've chosen, where working out aggressively on a machine turns into healing.

The alternate reality with the timer also wants to know when I'm going to acknowledge that my experiment has run its course and come up wanting. I can't answer that. Someone had to invent the light bulb, and we're all glad he did, never mind how many iterations it took him. How would I ever know if I've tried all the possibilities of my experiment, tweaked it in all the ways it might be tweaked?

In the video I say, "I don't have to get motivated to do this. I run from here [tapping my chest]. That's what impossible feels like That's what your impossible would feel like." All the research in the world won't give you that.

How long should you try?
Until.
Jim Rohn

I'm in this until. Pretty simple.

In the video, the guy behind the camera asks me if my experiment is working, and I admit it's not. Because of that, I wondered out loud one of our planning sessions whether doing the video was worth it. He brushed my hesitation aside. "Everybody needs inspiration," he said. End of discussion.

So the timer ticks away in its alternate reality, while I keep working out in this one. I get a lot of benefits from doing this. Discipline. Perseverance. Amazing overall good health. Not to mention lots of material to blog about and use in my workshops. Plus the joy of trying to hit a training goal that has me sweating buckets and willing my errant foot back into line, then finishing and barely making it to a nearby chair to sit down and massage the feeling back into my feet. If I quit, I'd miss all that. Honest.

But I'd trade it all for a walk around the block with my wife.

KILLING THEM SOFTLY
(PART ONE)

The Attack on Lawyers' Brains

I borrowed the title of this series from a Loyola Law Journal article by DU Law professor Debra S. Austin, J.D., Ph.D.: *Killing Them Softly: Neuroscience Reveals How Brain Cells Die From Law School Stress And How Neural Self-Hacking Can Optimize Cognitive Performance.*

The phrase "neural self-hacking" comes from Google, which runs a class for employees by that name, plus other classes on brain well-being. Yeah, it's a Silicon Valley thing, but don't be fooled: the companies offering these classes mean business, and they think mindfulness is good for it. As Prof. Austin says:

> Many innovative companies promote wellness to provide vibrant workplaces and thriving employees. Research shows that perks such as onsite gyms, work/life balance

programs, stress management classes, mindfulness training, and nutrition coaching improve the bottom line.

Killing Them Softly makes the case for why the law profession might want to catch up with that idea, instead of mounting a systematic attack on law students' and lawyers' brains. Prof. Austin's article describes in detail just how we do that, and the implications of this practice. Consider these excerpts:

> Neuroscience shows that the aggregate educative effects of training to become a lawyer under chronically stressful conditions may undermine the efforts of legal educators by weakening the learning capacities of law students. Stress in legal education may also set the stage for abnormally high rates of anxiety and depression among lawyers.
>
> The stresses facing law students and lawyers result in a significant decline in their well-being, including anxiety, panic attacks, depression, substance abuse, and suicide. Neuroscience now shows that this level of stress also diminishes cognitive capacity. The intricate workings of the brain, the ways in which memories become part of a lawyer's body of knowledge, and the impact of emotion on this process indicate that stress can weaken or kill brain cells needed for cognition.
>
> Cognition, Latin for "the faculty of knowing," describes the process by which humans perceive stimuli,

extract key information to hold in memory, and generate thoughts and actions to achieve goals.

In other words, the way we initiate lawyers into the profession and how we approach law practice is counterproductive on the most fundamental neurological level. We make it hard for lawyers' brains to do what we ask of them. We impede their ability to learn, to store knowledge and access memory, and to exercise sound judgment. Most critically, we restrict that essential lawyering ability to sort through the facts, discern what's important, and figure out what to do about it. And while we're at it, we also heighten susceptibility to the distressing psychological conditions that plague our profession.

And guess what? That's what happened to all of us. It's amazing any of us can function as our studies and work require, but our brains are amazingly resilient, and we'll talk about how they get the job done in the face of all this neurological aggression. Before we get that far, we'll look into how our brains learn, and how the stresses of the profession damage them. And we'll take a look at the case for neural self-hacking.

Stay tuned.

KILLING THEM SOFTLY
(PART TWO)

What Stress Does to the Brain

Stress in the law is a given. We know that from personal experience, but if we need more authority on the point, we needn't look further than the *2013 Colorado Lawyer Satisfaction and Salary Survey*, which reported that 94% of respondents said the law is stressful sometimes (48%), often (37%), or always (9%).

Brain scientist John Medina describes the impact of long-term chronic stress on the brain in his book *Brain Rules*:

> Stress hormones can do some truly nasty things to your brain if boatloads of the stuff are given free access to your central nervous system. That's what's going on when you experience chronic stress. Stress hormones seem to have a particular liking for cells

in the hippocampus, and that's problem, because the hippocampus is deeply involved in many aspects of human learning. Stress hormones can make cells in the hippocampus more vulnerable to other stresses. Stress hormones can disconnect neural networks, the webbing of brain cells that act like a safety deposit vault, storing your most precious memories. They can stop the hippocampus from giving birth to brand new baby neurons. Under extreme conditions, stress hormones can even kill hippocampus cells. Quite literally, severe stress can cause brain damage in the very tissues most likely to help your children pass their SATs.

The problem begins when too many stress hormones hang around in the brain too long, a situation you find in chronic stress, especially of the learned helplessness variety. ... Like a fortress overrun by invaders, enough stress hormones will overwhelm the brain's natural defenses and wreak their havoc. In sufficient quantities, stress hormones are fully capable of turning off the gene that makes [counter-stress hormones] in hippocampus cells. You read that right: Not only can they overwhelm our defenses, they can actually turn them off. The damaging effects can be long-lasting, a fact clearly observed when people experience catastrophic stress.

"Clearly, stress hurts learning," Prof. Medina concludes. "Most important, however, stress hurts people."

Some of the people stress hurts are law students and lawyers. Prof. Austin's *Killing Them Softly* article talks about the specific stresses of law school:

> The stresses of attending law school are legendary. After peppering seventy-five first year law students with questions about their experiences in their 1L year at the University of Memphis law school, Andrew J. McClurg asked students about their dominant feeling at the end of the year. The answers were disproportionately focused on anxiety and stress. Students reported grave concerns over upcoming finals, grades, and failing law school. They described suffering from "sheer, unrelenting exhaustion" and a "level of mental exhaustion I did not know existed."
>
> Four of the six universally recognized emotions are negative: fear, anger, sadness, and disgust. Stress involves some combination of these adverse emotions. Stress, a concept borrowed from engineering, "can be defined as the amount of resistance a material offers to being reshaped and reformed." If too great a load is placed on the beam supporting a structure or the law student trying to learn the law, it/he is damaged or collapses.
>
> When stress persists for a few hours or days, a law student may experience a bad mood. Longer-term stress can cause stress-related disorders such as panic attacks, anxiety, or depression; the physical effects include increased blood pressure, heart palpitations,

breathlessness, dizziness, irritability, chest pain, abdominal discomfort, sweating, chills, or increased muscle tension. These symptoms are caused by the stress response originating in the emotional brain.

Next time, we'll talk more about how stress hurts the people who study and practice law.

KILLING THEM SOFTLY
(PART THREE)

What Stress Does to People

I've been quoting extensively in this series from DU Law professor Debra Austin's *Killing Them Softly* article and neuroscientist John Medina's *Brain Rules* book. Let's hear more from both of them about what stress does to the people in the law profession.

Prof. Austin describes the impact of stress on cognition as follows:

> The impact of stress on law student cognition includes deterioration in memory, concentration, problem-solving, math performance, and language processing. Curiosity is dampened, and creativity is diminished. A paralysis sets in, limiting motivation and the ability to break out of repetitive behavior patterns.

Prof. Medina elaborates:

> If the stress is too severe or too prolonged, however, stress begins to harm learning. The influence can be devastating. ... Stressed people... don't do math very well. They don't process language very efficiently. They have poorer memories, both short and long forms.
>
> Stressed individuals do not generalize or adapt old pieces of information to new scenarios as well as non-stressed individuals. the can't concentrate. In almost every way it can be tested, chronic stress hurts our ability to learn.
>
> One study showed that adults with high stress levels performed 50 percent worse on certain cognitive tests than adults with low stress. Specifically, stress hurts declarative memory (things you can declare) and executive function (the type of thinking that involves problem solving).

Stress affects physiological wellbeing. From Prof Austin:

> Long-term elevated levels of glucocorticoids resulting from chronic stress have been associated with the following physical conditions:
>
> Impaired immune response;
> Increased appetite and food cravings;
> Increased body fat;

> Increased symptoms of PMS and menopause;
> Decreased muscle mass;
> Decreased bone density; and
> Decreased libido.

Stress also affects psychological wellbeing. Again from Prof. Austin:

> Chronic stress also produces the following emotional conditions:
>
> > Increased mood swings, irritability, and anger;
> > Increased anxiety; and
> > Increased depression.

Of particular concern to the law profession is the nexus between stress and depression. From Prof. Austion:

> Law is a cognitive profession, and the legendary stressors in legal education and the practice of law can take a tremendous toll on cognitive capacity. Lawyers suffer from depression at triple the rate of non-lawyers.

Again, Prof. Medina elaborates:

> [Depression] is a disease every bit as organic as diabetes, and often deadlier. Chronic exposure to stress can lead you to depression's doorstep, then push you through.

[D]epression hobbles the brain's natural impro-
visatory instincts the way arthritis hobbles a dancer.
Fluid intelligence, problem-solving abilities (including
quantitative reasoning), and memory formation are
deeply affected by depression. The result is an erosion
of innovation and creativity, just as biochemically real
as if we were talking about joints and muscles.

Depression is a deregulation of thought processes,
including memory, language, quantitative thinking,
fluid intelligence, and spatial perception.

Depression not only impairs us in these ways, it creates
a perception that things will never get better. From Prof.
Medina:

This list [of depression's effects] is long and familiar.
But one of the hallmarks may not be as familiar, unless
you are in depression. Many people who feel depressed
also feel there is no way out of their depression. They
feel life's shocks are permanent and things will never
get better. Even when there is a way out -- treatment
is often very successful -- there is no perception of it.
They can no more argue their way out of depression
than they could argue their way out of a heart attack.

KILLING THEM SOFTLY
(PART FOUR)

Law School: Legally Inflicted Brain Damage

Law professor Douglas Litowitz's 2005 book *The Destruction of Young Lawyers* summarizes the law school experience this way:

> The one thing that we know with certainty about law school is that it *breaks* people, that it is experienced as a trauma, an assault. Like other traumas, when it is actually taking place it is overwhelming and very difficult to understand. Only after it is already finished can it be pieced together in retrospect, like a robbery victim who later tries to reconstruct the features of an assailant.
>
> When I say that law school *breaks* people, I mean that almost nobody comes out of law school feeling better about themselves, although many come out

much worse – caustic, paranoid, and overly competitive. From outward appearances, the students churned out by the law school machine are shiny and bright, with a professional no-nonsense attitude, but inside that shell lies a nagging hollowness.

Law school is not transformative because it does not engage the students on an emotional or intellectual level.

Strong words indeed, but nine years after Prof. Litowitz wrote them, Prof. Austin's *Killing Them Softly* article reveals that we've got a lot of new neuroscience to back them up, or in some cases clarify them. For example, Prof. Austin points out that it's not that law school doesn't engage the emotions, but that it does so through a filter of stress:

The intricate workings of the brain, the ways in which memories become part of a lawyer's body of knowledge, and *the impact of emotion on this process* indicate that stress can weaken or kill brain cells needed for cognition. (Emphasis added.)

Stressed emotions warp neural function, debilitating and even destroying the very brain processes needed to achieve what Prof. Austin calls "optimal cognitive fitness." She thinks we can do better:

Because the processes of learning, memory storage, and memory retrieval involve both the emotional and thinking brains, law students, legal educators, and law-yers should develop an understanding of the impact of emotion on cognition and the nexus between brain and body.

In other words, if we could get our minds around the idea that promoting law student brain and body wellness would be good for all of us, we would approach legal learning in way that, instead of traumatizing law students, would enhance their learning and improve their overall health. In fact, we would emphasize helping law students be *happy* about studying law.

A prior blog post said this about promoting happiness in law practice:

> [H]appy lawyers are more likely to deliver the best of the competence, communication, timeliness, and sound judgment we're ethically obligated to provide. It also means that the best-performing law firms – the firms that will also make the "best places to work" lists – could be founded on a single guiding principle: promote law-yer happiness.

The same could be true of law schools.

Now *there's* a concept....

KILLING THEM SOFTLY
(PART FIVE)

Rethinking the Holy Grail

The Holy Grail of legal education has long been teaching law students to "think like a lawyer." Most of us have a vague sense of what that means and how it's accomplished, but turns out it's an actual brain process known to neuroscientists as *conditioning*. Linda Graham's book *Bouncing Back: Rewiring Your Brain For Maximum Resilience and Well-Being* describes conditioning as follows:

> Conditioning creates automatic habits of behavior by encoding the neural firing patterns of repeated responses to experience, stabilizing the neural circuitry of that learning, and storing those patterns of response in implicit (unconscious) memory. When you repeat a pattern of behavior often enough, eventually you don't

have to focus your attention on it anymore; the neural circuits underlying that behavior have stabilized in your brain, enabling you to respond to a similar situation automatically.

Creating habits of behavior through conditioning is your brain's way of being efficient. Without conditioning, you'd have to relearn how to tie your shoes every morning....

[F]ocused attention causes neurons in the brain to fire; focusing on the same object or experience causes repeated neural firings; and repeated neural firings create new and stable neural structure. When we focus our attention on cultivating a particular pattern of behavior, a character trait, or attitude or lens for filtering experience, we incline the mind toward that objective... We notice more readily the desired trait or behavior, register it more fully in our consciousness, and direct mental activity toward it,

[W]hen we formulate an intention..., the repeated focus on that intention begins to build new brain structure and circuitry that support us... We turn a neural goat path into a freeway.

Thus the Holy Grail is pursued and realized. For three years, we condition law students' brains, turning their lawyer-like neural goat paths (remember what it was like the first time you read a case or a contract?) into neural freeways (consider how you read them now).

No problem if that's all that happened, but combine brain conditioning with the brain damage caused by law school stress, and ironically, it appears that too often we accomplish this educational ideal by turning out lawyers who all think in the same brain-damaged way. *The Destruction of Young Lawyers* describes this outcome as follows:

> At the same time that law school *breaks* students, it also *creates* them, or rather, molds them in its image. But what does it create? On the positive side it creates people who have good reading and writing skills, who are diligent and hardworking, who can see both sides to an issue. Law students are hard workers, and they are typically very high achievers with above-average intelligence.
>
> But on another level, law school churns out some very scared people…. [A]t the same time that [law students] are taught to act empowered, they are truly disempowered… Despite the appearance of professionalism and self-sufficiency, law students are actually helpless and dependent when they graduate.

Thankfully, there is an antidote. *Bouncing Back* introduces it:

> If conditioning is the process that encodes stable patterns in our neural circuitry, neuroplasticity is the mechanism that works to alter them.

As Prof. Austin says in *Killing Them Softly*:

> The modification of neural networks in response to experience, such as legal education, is neuroplasticity.

Neuroplasticity is why some (not all) lawyers' brains and hearts recover from law school and avoid the impact of law practice stress.

More next time.

KILLING THEM SOFTLY
(PART SIX)

Bouncing Back

The reason not all law students and lawyers are paralyzed with stress-induced brain damage is because our brains are resilient. They bounce back. They successfully resist or unlearn stress conditioning.

Stress is profession-wide, but adaptation to stressful experience, including resistance and recovery, is individual by individual. As Prof. Austin explains in *Killing Them Softly*:

> The brains of all healthy law students are comprised of the triune structure: the primitive, emotional, and thinking brains. The critical unit of communication within each brain is the tree-shaped neuron, which relies on the electrochemical process of transmitting information through the brain and between brain

and body. Every law student has a multitude of neuronal networks operating within the brain. But each student's transit system map of neuron data pathways, referred to as the connectome, is unique.

"You are your synapses," and your brain is a "work in progress" because your connectome is continuously rewiring itself. The brain is in a constant state of change. It has the capacity to produce new neurons in the hippocampus and the olefactory bulbs (parts of the emotional brain) in a process called neurogenesis. The modification of neural networks in response to experience, such as legal education, is neuroplasticity.

Linda Graham's book *Bouncing Back* describes neuroplasticity this way:

> Technically, neuroplasticity is the lifelong capacity of the brain to create new neurons (brain cells) and connections among neurons (neural pathways and circuits)... When you focus attention on the conditioned pattern you want to rewire, you activate the neural networks of that pattern and cause the neurons to fire again. When you know how to harness the neuroplasticity of your brain in that moment, you can alter the pattern.

In other words, neuroplasticity isn't just something that happens in the normal course of life inside our skulls, it's also a skill we can consciously practice to our advantage. As Prof. Austin points out, "The brains of law students and lawyers are continuously being rewired and everything they do, think, and feel is governed by their neural networks." We can either allow this to happen without our conscious intent, and leave the prospect of suffering brain damage and recovering from it up to chance, or we can engage in the intentional "neural self-hacking" Prof. Austin advocates -- a term taken from "a class taught at Google, [that] teaches employees about the power of neuroplasticity."

Using neuroplasticity to our benefit is a skill we can either use or lose. As Prof. Austin says,

> The brain has the power to change itself through the personal effort and choices of its owner. Brain plasticity is competitive; we keep the skills we practice and we lose the ones we do not.

Embracing this skill requires focus and perseverance. As *Bouncing Back* says:

> All mental activity creates neural structure. Using neuroplasticity to strengthen brain structures is like working out at the gym to build up our muscles. (Of course, the structures of the brain aren't actually muscles; they're densely networked circuits and pathways of neurons. But strengthening the capacities of these neurons to communicate with one another, and to integrate the information being processed into new responses, is comparable to working out to strengthen our muscles.)

Perseverance in our efforts to harness neuroplasticity is the sine qua non of rewiring our brains. By persevering in the use of new tools and techniques, we are stabilizing the new neural circuitry so that it can serve as a reliable platform of resilient behavior, not easily overridden by the pulls of the past.

Frequent and regular repetition creates steady neural firing and rewiring and accelerates the process. ... [A] stance of willingness -- focusing on possibilities -- is more effective than a stance of willpower -- focusing on performance. It almost doesn't matter how small the increment of change is.

What's important is that we choose practices that catalyze positive change and that we persevere.

We'll look at one of those catalytic practices next time.

KILLING THEM SOFTLY
(PART SEVEN)

The Ethics of Mindfulness
And Why it Works

Prof. Austin's *Killing Them Softly* article reminds us that not only can we help ourselves to overcome legally-inflicted brain (and heart) damage, *we have an ethical duty to do so*:

> Each law student, law professor, and lawyer has the power to alter brain processes to achieve states more conducive to learning.
>
> Rule 1.1 of the American Bar Association Model Rules of Professional Conduct requires lawyers to be competent in completing their duties on behalf of their clients. Law students, law professors, and lawyers can benefit from developing a neuroscience-based understanding of how to optimize their own cognition.

If we're willing, neuroscience can help us take up the challenge to operate at a higher cognitive and ethical level:

> Developments in neuroscience identify areas of cognition in the brain and indicate recommendations that enhance cognitive effectiveness, performance, and productivity. Steps taken to increase cognitive fitness can strengthen lawyer creativity and well-being.
>
> Knowledge of these neuroscience findings will empower law students, law professors, and lawyers to enhance their cognitive wellness.
>
> Law schools and law firms, like many cutting-edge companies, can curate a culture of cognitive wellness.

Promoting cognitive wellness is good health, good ethics, and good business. As for the latter:

> In addition to bolstering cognitive competence, cognitive wellness initiatives may also provide a lawyer with a competitive advantage.
>
> Many innovative companies promote wellness to provide vibrant workplaces and thriving employees. Research shows that perks such as onsite gyms, work/ life balance programs, stress management classes, mindfulness training, and nutrition coaching improve the bottom line.

If we're not doing this already, then where do we start? According to Prof. Austin, with mindfulness training:

The best cognitive approach to dealing with stress is mindfulness. Research on mindfulness indicates that it: strengthens the insula in the thinking brain (the early detection system of well-being);

increases gray matter and connections between brain regions;

improves immune function;

decreases distraction; and

equips the brain to notice patterns and events before responses become overly-reactive.

Mindfulness works as an antidote to cognitive impairment because it bypasses our habitual cognitive processes. Mindfulness doesn't ask us to think, analyze, reason, argue, and high achieve our way into a stress-free mindset. Instead, it shifts our brains to a new state of perception and awareness, where we can make behavioral choices that alter the ethos of stress itself. In fact, mindfulness is not about thinking at all:

> [M]indfulness is attention without labels, ideas, thoughts, or opinions. Mindfulness means "being fully aware of something" and paying attention to the moment, with acceptance and without judgment or resistance. It requires "emotion-introspection rather than cognitive self-reflection," and specifically does not involve the analysis of thoughts or feelings. Mindfulness is a form of self-understanding involving self-awareness rather than thinking.

Practiced with intention and perseverance, mindfulness is just what the brain (and heart) doctor ordered:

> Mindfulness improves information processing and decision-making. It provides space between awareness, and judgments and reactions, which may encourage the onset of flow. Flow is a term coined by psychologist Mihaly Csikszentmihalyi to describe the state of effortless concentration when humans are so engaged in a task they lose track of time.
>
> Being mindful allows you to have control over your attention so that you can place it where you want and shift it to something else when you want to. When attention is steady, it cannot be appropriated by whatever intrudes on awareness, but remains grounded and stable. Developing greater control over attention is a powerful way for law students and lawyers to sculpt their brains.

Mindfulness is not just a powerful way to sculpt our brains, but our careers and our profession as well.

More on that next time, and then this series is over.

KILLING THEM SOFTLY
(PART EIGHT)

What We Might Be Missing

The Abstract to Prof. Austin's *Killing Them Softly* states that "This Article provides a groundbreaking synthesis on the neuroscience of achieving optimal cognitive fitness for all law students, law professors, and lawyers." The article is all that, and more: it's also a call to action.

Killing Them Softly looks at issues such as legal ethics and the cognitive performance and general wellbeing of law students and lawyers through the lens of neuroscience. What we see through that lens invites us to change -- assuming we don't like the idea that we're inflicting brain damage on ourselves and each other.

Strange, though, isn't it, but articles like this are rarely incendiary. They get read and cited, they prompt dialogue, and then the wheels of change roll slowly through institutions, grinding against a powerful ethos of "this is the way we've always done it." Eventually change happens, but it's not exactly a forest fire.

What we might be missing is that the market for legal products and services isn't constrained by institutional sluggishness, and is already running ahead, embracing change. The market isn't hidebound, it can move as fast as it wants. And if it wants something other than lawyers thinking through a cognitive fog, it can get it. Now.

Presumably, there will always be a need for lawyers who can "think like a lawyer" that way the ideal was originally intended, but nowadays that's a shrinking market segment. A sizeable and burgeoning market segment has already broken off that apparently doesn't want lawyers who think like lawyers -- at least, not in those brain-damaged, cognitively impaired ways we've been looking at in this series. That segment has already found a way to buy *legal commodities delivered by non-lawyers* that used to be *delivered as services by lawyers*. (This blog catalogued some of these developments earlier this year. *See Future Shock and the Business of Law, The New Lawyer Entrepreneurs*, and *Learning to Think Like a Lawyer and Entrepreneur*.)

Saying "but they're not supposed to do that" is a finger in the dike. Worldwide ecommerce wants what it wants when it wants it, and the fastest market responders are all over mindfulness and wellness as a business growth strategy. If they so choose, those are the people who will develop a new market segment of law schools and law

LAW, ENLIGHTENMENT, AND OTHER STATES OF MIND

practices operating at "optimal cognitive fitness" and fostering "achievement cultures," as Prof. Austin advocates.

Now *that's* incendiary change. If we want in on it, the resources are out there. Again, from Prof. Austin:

> One of the most supportive achievement workplace cultures can be found at Google. The master of ceremonies, and developer of Google's Search Inside Yourself (SIY) emotional intelligence curriculum, is Chade-Meng Tan. The benefits of developing emotional intelligence competence include strong work performance, excellent leadership skills, and the capacity for sustainable happiness.

For more about SIY, check out the *Inside Yourself Leadership Institute* website. Here's their mission statement:

> We develop effective, innovative leaders using science-backed mindfulness and emotional intelligence training.

The World of Woo-Woo has taken up residence on Wall Street. The legal profession might want to join them. Prof. Austin issues the invitation:

> Neural self-hacking is likely to be the newest fitness movement and law students, law professors, and lawyers should be among the early adopters of a regimen of cognitive wellness.

Early adopters? The legal profession?

It could happen.

(The concept of "emotional intelligence" originated in Daniel Coleman's book by that name.)

ॐ

A SPECIAL THANKS

This is from the Denver Bar Association's website:

> The Waterman Fund is a charitable trust that provides financial assistance to Colorado lawyers. The trust was created by the will of Anna Waterman, surviving spouse of Colorado's U.S. Senator, Charles Waterman.
>
> Financial awards from the Fund are made "...for the sole and only purpose of relieving the financial necessities, assuaging the hardships and lightening the financial burdens of aged, infirm or otherwise incapacitated members of the Colorado bar, in good repute and standing, and who shall have practiced law in Colorado for a period of at least 10 years...."

I'm a beneficiary of the Fund.

As Ron Sandgrund has written, I've made a joke out of my foibles getting in and out of the law. It's true, my ineptitude *is* funny. It's also true that, mainly for the reasons described in the three "Running Past Our Limits" series collected in this book, the law practice doesn't work for me anymore. Not for lack of trying.

As a result, I was scrambling to find my financial feet earlier this year. About then, I met with Barbara Ezyk and Sarah Myers of the Colorado Lawyer Assistance Fund to get some material for my *Winds of Change* series. A couple weeks later, I reached out again: "Um, maybe COLAP could help me?" Barbara referred me to the Waterman Fund, I applied, and the administrators provided me with a stipend to cover basic living costs.

Among other things, that stipend freed me to dive into my new career as a writer. The first order of business was to create a body of work. I've been on it. This book, the two listed below, and a fourth book currently in progress were all made possible by that stipend. (My book *Life Beyond Reason* was already written, but it still needed to be published and promoted.)

I'm good with words, but they fail me when I try to express my gratitude for Anna Waterman's and the fund administrators' gift to me and others like me. I've made a personal commitment to pay it forward from the proceeds of this book.

Just wanted you to know.

Kevin Rhodes
October 2014

ABOUT THE AUTHOR, LINKS

Thank you for reading my book! If you enjoyed it, would you kindly consider taking a moment to leave a review?
Thanks!
Kevin

Connect With Me

For all my links, and for a contact me form, go to the "Links" and "Connect" pages of my website at **www.kevin-rhodes.com.**

www.ingramcontent.com/pod-product-compliance
Lightning Source LLC
Chambersburg PA
CBHW050502210326
41521CB00011B/2294